The Birder's Journal

Second Edition

0 11557 02697 9

The
Birder's Journal

Second Edition

Mel M. Baughman

Illustrations by Nell E. Fronabarger

STACKPOLE
BOOKS

First published in 1989 in hardcover under the title *The Birder's Journal*, by The Baughman Company

Printed in the United States of America

10 9 8 7 6 5 4 3 2 1

Second edition

Cover design by Caroline Stover

To Oleta Becker,
who taught me to see the fossils in the
rocks, and to know the shape of an
arrowhead lying among the shards of
an ancient people; who showed me the
sanctuary of the wilderness and the
perfection of all the creatures in it; for
instilling a reverence for knowledge
and showing me the need for gentle-
ness, but especially for giving the most
precious gift of all, her time.

CONTENTS

PREFACE

Bird-watching is always an adventure, whether we are sitting at a window enjoying the familiar visitors to our gardens and feeders, or packing our equipment into duffels and grabbing our passports to disappear into the bush. Our passion is one of great dimensions, making physical demands on our bodies in the field, and offering mental, even intellectual rewards for time spent with the books in the comfort of our studies. And it is even more rewarding when we share our passion with others. For what more is life, really, but hard work, hard thinking, and warm fellowship? Bird-watching, too, is a lifetime of study and safari with fine friends.

During the seven years since *The Birder's Journal* was published in paperback by Stackpole Books, bird names have changed, ranges have changed, species designations have been altered by the American Ornithological Union (AOU), and even a few new birds have been added to those living and breeding in North America.

These combined changes created enough impact on the list of birds we have the opportunity of seeing in the field that we felt it was time to revise and update *The Birder's Journal*. To this end, we have added over 250 birds to the book, so no matter what bird you may see afield, it is very likely represented in these pages. All common and scientific names are current with the 1998 seventh edition of the AOU's *Checklist of North American Birds*.

Your new field journal is still the perfect place to record and maintain your life list. The essential companion to your *Birder's Journal* is your field guide, such as the National Geographic Society's *Field Guide to the Birds of North America*, third edition.

I hope your new *Birder's Journal* adds greatly to your lifelong birding experience, and may all your time afield be memorable.

Mel Baughman

COLORING TIPS

From the artist who sketched the birds in *The Birder's Journal*:

My copy of *The Birder's Journal* is very important to me. I treasure it as an invaluable record of the time I've spent bird-watching, and I hope you'll come to feel the same about your copy.

As you use the book, in addition to jotting down notes about the place, date, and situation for each bird you identify, I want to encourage you to illustrate the sketches by highlighting at least the major field markings of each bird you see. Colored pencil is probably the best medium to use for this. A small set of pencils is easy to carry, and the colors do not smear. I recommend Berol Prismacolor pencils—the colors are brilliant and long lasting.

Here are some tips I discovered in coloring my copy of *The Birder's Journal*:
• Keep pencil points sharp for control in detail.
• Color in the direction in which the bird's feathers lie, rather than in a circular motion.
• Use light pressure for softer colors and slightly heavier pressure for a more solid color—but remember that too much pressure can tear the paper.
• Create more realistic blends of color and add shading details by layering one color over another.
• Use a white pencil, or simply leave the paper exposed, to create highlights such as catch-lights in the eyes.
• Choose colors carefully—once on paper, they cannot be completely removed. They can be lightened by lifting some of the pigment with a kneaded eraser, then use the pencil eraser.
• Note that each bird has been drawn with hatch marks to indicate a change or transition in color.

You are ready for an exciting and enjoyable day in the field with your copy of *The Birder's Journal*, your pencils, and a sharpener. Most birders also carry a camera. Photographs are a great help, as are the illustrations in your field guide, if you want to add more detail to the bird drawings.

Nell Fronabarger

Loons
(family Gaviidae)

It was a cool September night. I stood on the bank of Ontario's Albany River and listened to the cold, dark water tumble through a series of pools as it moved inexorably to the Hudson Bay. The northern lights fired the sky, veiling the starlight. A loon flew through the darkness on its way back in time. I shivered as I heard its lonely, primordial song. All was timeless. Loon song. Eternity.

Red-throated Loon
Gavia stellata

Date of Sighting

Location of Sighting

Notes

Pacific Loon
Gavia pacifica

Date of Sighting

Location of Sighting

Notes

Arctic Loon
Gavia arctica

Date of Sighting
_____

Location of Sighting
_____

Notes
_____
_____
_____
_____
_____
_____
_____
_____
_____

Common Loon
Gavia immer

Date of Sighting
_____

Location of Sighting
_____

Notes
_____
_____
_____
_____
_____
_____
_____
_____

Yellow-billed Loon

Gavia adamsii

Date of Sighting

Location of Sighting

Notes

Grebes
(family Podicipedidae)

Master submariners and strong swimmers, grebes seem to be more at home in and on the water than in the air. Their rear-set legs and strong, lobed toes propel them underwater at speeds fast enough to chase down small fish.

Horned Grebe
Podiceps auritus

Date of Sighting

Location of Sighting

Notes

Eared Grebe
Podiceps nigricollis

Date of Sighting

Location of Sighting

Notes

Pied-billed Grebe
Podilymbus podiceps

Date of Sighting

Location of Sighting

Notes

Least Grebe
Tachybaptus dominicus

Date of Sighting

Location of Sighting

Notes

Red-necked Grebe
Podiceps grisegena

Date of Sighting

Location of Sighting

Notes

Clark's Grebe
Aechmophorus clarkii

Date of Sighting

Location of Sighting

Notes

Western Grebe

Aechmophorus occidentalis

Date of Sighting

Location of Sighting

Notes

Albatrosses
(family Diomedeidae)

These largest of all seabirds are also among the most long-lived birds, living perhaps fifty or more years. Their long, high-aspect-ratio wing design makes albatrosses the finest gliders on earth. They are such competent fliers that some believe they may even sleep on the wing. These elegant, mythic seabirds mate for life and begin breeding barely before their tenth year, laying only one egg approximately every other year. Worldwide their population is in decline. Thousands die each year, dragged to their deaths when they attempt to feed on the squid baited to the hooks of longline fishermen. Generally, going to sea is the only way to view this magnificent family of seabirds.

Short-tailed Albatross
Phoebastria albatrus

Date of Sighting

Location of Sighting

Notes

Shy Albatross
Thalassarche cauta

Date of Sighting

Location of Sighting

Notes

Laysan Albatross
Phoebastria immutabilis

Date of Sighting

Location of Sighting

Notes

Black-footed Albatross
Phoebastria nigripes

Date of Sighting

Location of Sighting

Notes

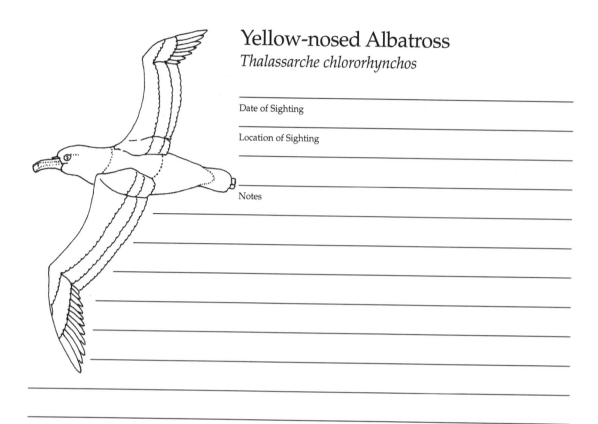

Yellow-nosed Albatross
Thalassarche chlororhynchos

Date of Sighting

Location of Sighting

Notes

Black-browed Albatross
Thalassarche melanophris

Date of Sighting

Location of Sighting

Notes

Shearwaters and Petrels

(family Procellariidae)

The family of shearwaters and petrels is related to albatrosses, but these smaller seabirds are not stately gliders. They are fast fliers, most often seen skimming the wave tops so closely that they regularly shear the water with a wingtip. Our knowledge of this family of seabirds is rapidly expanding because of the long-term dedication of a handful of pelagic birders on both coasts. Take a pelagic birding cruise with an expert "sea-birder" to really get to know these beauties.

Northern Fulmar
Fulmarus glacialis

Date of Sighting

Location of Sighting

Notes

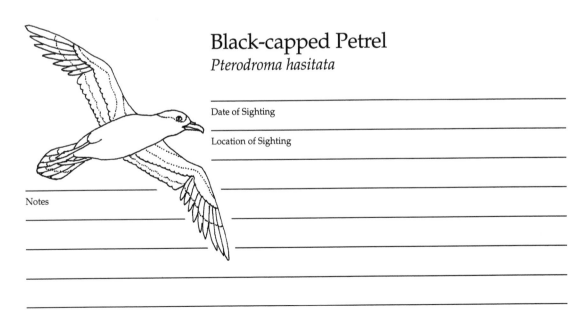

Black-capped Petrel
Pterodroma hasitata

Date of Sighting

Location of Sighting

Notes

Fea's Petrel
Pterodroma feae

Date of Sighting

Location of Sighting

Notes

Bermuda Petrel
Pterodroma cahow

Date of Sighting

Location of Sighting

Notes

Herald Petrel
Pterodroma arminjoniana

Date of Sighting

Location of Sighting

Notes

Dark-rumped Petrel
Pterodroma phaeopygia

Date of Sighting

Location of Sighting

Notes

Murphy's Petrel
Pterodroma ultima

Date of Sighting

Location of Sighting

Notes

Mottled Petrel
Pterodroma inexpectata

Date of Sighting

Location of Sighting

Notes

Cook's Petrel
Pterodroma cookii

Date of Sighting

Location of Sighting

Notes

Stejneger's Petrel
Pterodroma longirostris

Date of Sighting

Location of Sighting

Notes

Streaked Shearwater
Calonectris leucomelas

Date of Sighting

Location of Sighting

Notes

Buller's Shearwater
Puffinus bulleri

Date of Sighting

Location of Sighting

Notes

Pink-footed Shearwater
Puffinus creatopus

Date of Sighting

Location of Sighting

Notes

Black-vented Shearwater
Puffinus opisthomelas

Date of Sighting

Location of Sighting

Notes

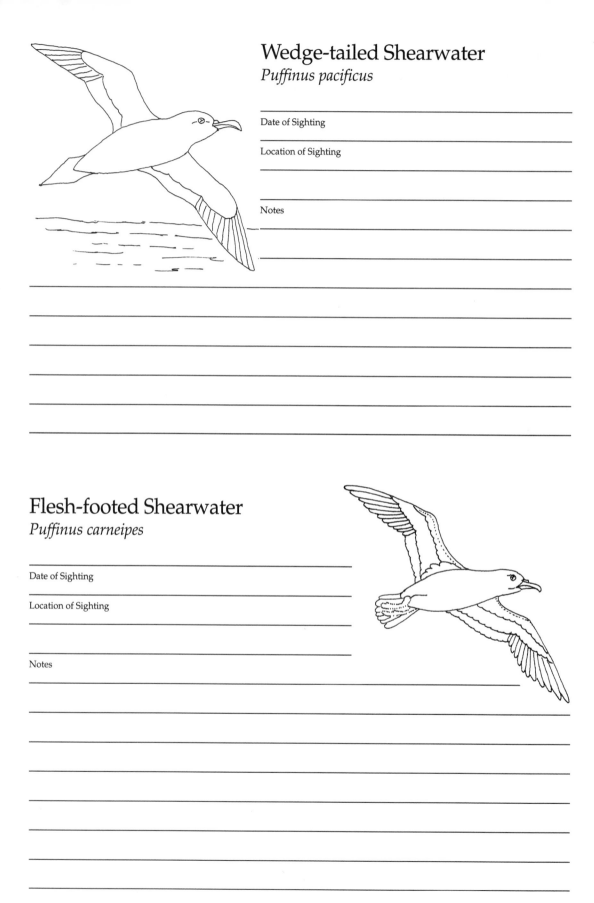

Wedge-tailed Shearwater
Puffinus pacificus

Date of Sighting

Location of Sighting

Notes

Flesh-footed Shearwater
Puffinus carneipes

Date of Sighting

Location of Sighting

Notes

Bulwer's Petrel
Bulweria bulwerii

Date of Sighting

Location of Sighting

Notes

Short-tailed Shearwater
Puffinus tenuirostris

Date of Sighting

Location of Sighting

Notes

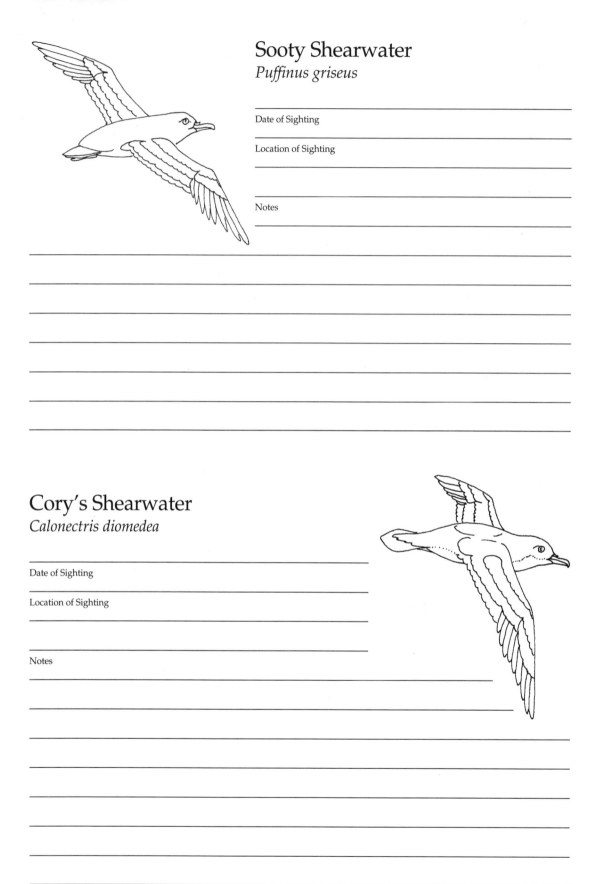

Sooty Shearwater
Puffinus griseus

Date of Sighting

Location of Sighting

Notes

Cory's Shearwater
Calonectris diomedea

Date of Sighting

Location of Sighting

Notes

Greater Shearwater
Puffinus gravis

Date of Sighting

Location of Sighting

Notes

Manx Shearwater
Puffinus puffinus

Date of Sighting

Location of Sighting

Notes

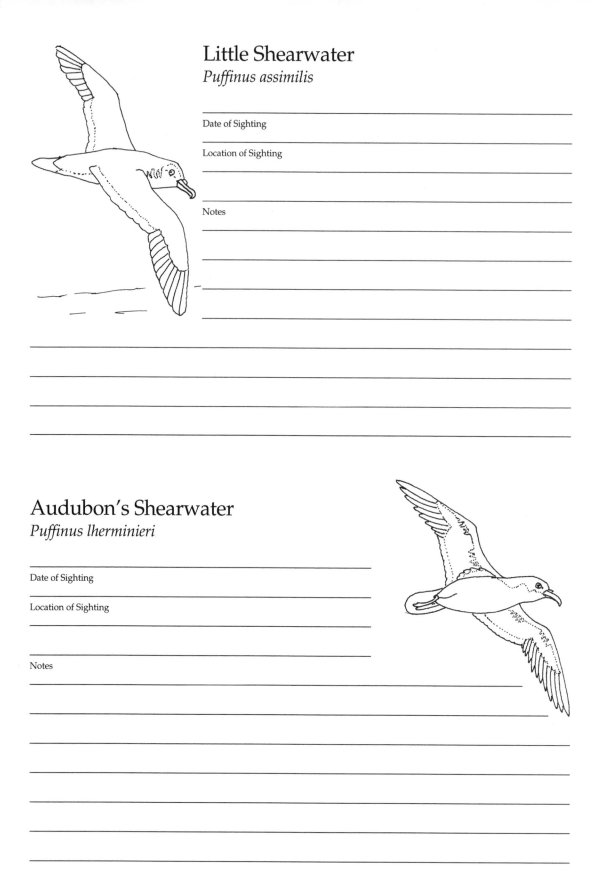

Little Shearwater
Puffinus assimilis

Date of Sighting

Location of Sighting

Notes

Audubon's Shearwater
Puffinus lherminieri

Date of Sighting

Location of Sighting

Notes

Storm-Petrels
(family Hydrobatidae)

Storm-petrels are the ballerinas of the pelagic world, fluttering like butterflies and daintily pattering the surface of the water with their feet as they search for food. So small, about the size of thrushes, and tricky to identify—one must go to the sea with an expert to help with the subtleties of storm-petrel field identification.

Wilson's Storm-Petrel
Oceanites oceanicus

Date of Sighting

Location of Sighting

Notes

Band-rumped Storm-Petrel
Oceanodroma castro

Date of Sighting

Location of Sighting

Notes

Leach's Storm-Petrel
Oceanodroma leucorhoa

Date of Sighting

Location of Sighting

Notes

White-faced Storm-Petrel
Pelagodroma marina

Date of Sighting

Location of Sighting

Notes

Black Storm-Petrel
Oceanodroma melania

Date of Sighting

Location of Sighting

Notes

Ashy Storm-Petrel
Oceanodroma homochroa

Date of Sighting

Location of Sighting

Notes

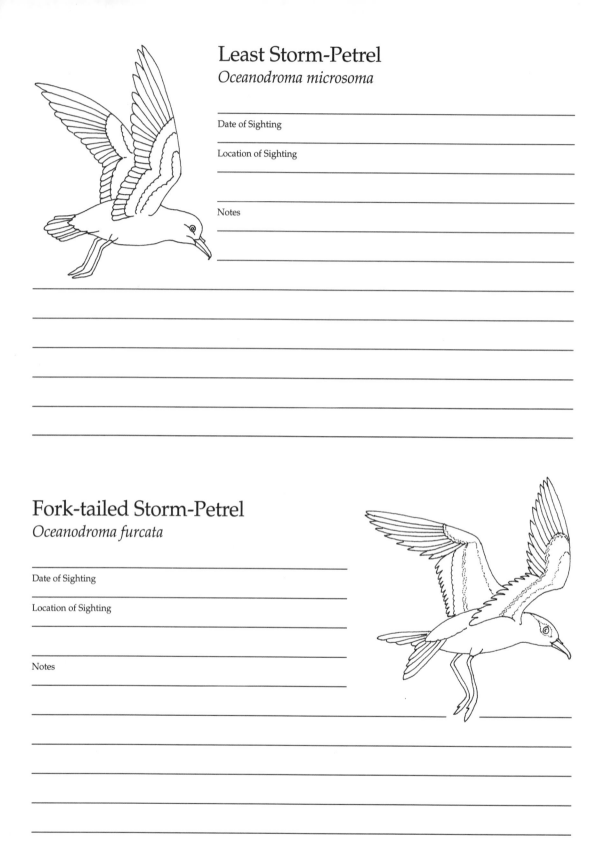

Least Storm-Petrel
Oceanodroma microsoma

Date of Sighting

Location of Sighting

Notes

Fork-tailed Storm-Petrel
Oceanodroma furcata

Date of Sighting

Location of Sighting

Notes

Wedge-rumped Storm-Petrel
Oceanodroma tethys

Date of Sighting

Location of Sighting

Notes

Frigatebirds

(family Fregatidae)

The Magnificent Frigatebird is fascinating in many ways. The total weight of its feathers is more than the total weight of its bones. Its seven-foot-plus wingspan is greater in ratio to its weight than is any other bird's. They feed by snatching food from the surface of the water, or by strafing other birds, forcing them to drop their food, then swooping to snatch it in mid-air. Magnificent Frigatebirds are most common along the Florida and Gulf coasts.

Magnificent Frigatebird

Fregata magnificens

Date of Sighting

Location of Sighting

Notes

Tropicbirds
(family Phaethontidae)

Of all the seabirds, the tropicbirds may be the most beautiful—in elegant dress with long streamer tails, a touch of color on their beaks, and patterns of dark feathers contrasting with the overall white of their bodies. You will most likely see these birds off the coast of Hawaii and the Dry Tortugas, although the White-tailed Tropicbird is seen with some regularity during the summer off the coast of North Carolina.

White-tailed Tropicbird
Phaethon lepturus

Date of Sighting

Location of Sighting

Notes

Red-billed Tropicbird
Phaethon aethereus

Date of Sighting

Location of Sighting

Notes

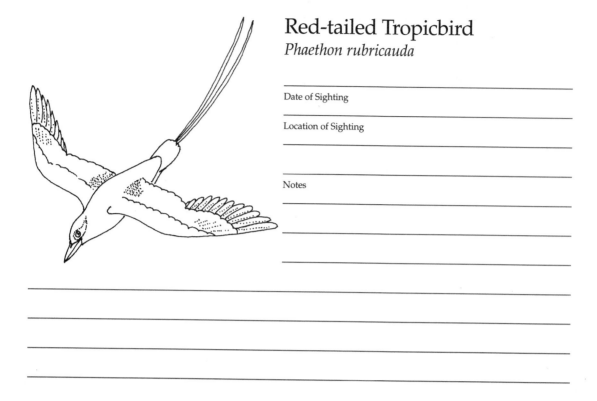

Red-tailed Tropicbird
Phaethon rubricauda

Date of Sighting

Location of Sighting

Notes

Boobies and Gannets

(family Sulidae)

Sportsfishermen rejoice when they spot a concentration of these expert fish-finders. When a school of tuna surrounds a school of bait fish, boobies and gannets seem to be the first to know. They flock above the bait fish, which are driven to the surface to escape the tuna below. Squadrons of seabirds tightly fold their wings and dive from above, spearing into the fish at great speed. Witnessing this feeding frenzy is one of the great spectacles of the high seas.

Red-footed Booby
Sula sula

Date of Sighting

Location of Sighting

Notes

Brown Booby
Sula leucogaster

Date of Sighting

Location of Sighting

Notes

Blue-footed Booby
Sula nebouxii

Date of Sighting

Location of Sighting

Notes

Masked Booby
Sula dactylatra

Date of Sighting

Location of Sighting

Notes

Northern Gannet
Morus bassanus

Date of Sighting

Location of Sighting

Notes

Pelicans
(family Pelecanidae)

The American White Pelican, with its nine-foot wingspan and five-foot length, is the largest bird in North America. This big bird has a rather gentle feeding approach, simply dipping its beak to "net" fish into its pouch as it swims along the surface of the water. The smaller Brown Pelican, on the other hand, plunges headlong into the water to trap fish with it huge, expandable bucketlike beak.

American White Pelican
Pelecanus erythrorhynchos

Date of Sighting

Location of Sighting

Notes

Brown Pelican
Pelecanus occidentalis

Date of Sighting

Location of Sighting

Notes

Darters
(family Anhingidae)

Our only North American darter is the reptilian Anhinga, known colloquially as the "snake-bird" for its habit of swimming with its body submerged and only its long, snaky neck and head above the surface of the water. The quintessential birder's view of the Anhinga is perched on a low branch in the mangroves, with its large black and white wings fully outstretched, drying in the sun.

Anhinga
Anhinga anhinga

Date of Sighting

Location of Sighting

Notes

Cormorants
(family Phalacrocoracidae)

We heap both verbal and physical abuse upon these poor birds. We call them ugly names like shite-poke and kill them by the hundreds when we feel they are competing with us as sportsfishermen. In reality, cormorants simply do what nature designed them to do best; they are experts at catching fish.

Neotropic Cormorant
Phalacrocorax brasilianus

Date of Sighting

Location of Sighting

Notes

Great Cormorant
Phalacrocorax carbo

Date of Sighting

Location of Sighting

Notes

Double-crested Cormorant
Phalacrocorax auritus

Date of Sighting

Location of Sighting

Notes

Brandt's Cormorant
Phalacrocorax penicillatus

Date of Sighting

Location of Sighting

Notes

Pelagic Cormorant
Phalacrocorax pelagicus

Date of Sighting

Location of Sighting

Notes

Red-faced Cormorant
Phalacrocorax urile

Date of Sighting

Location of Sighting

Notes

Bitterns, Herons, and Egrets

(family Ardeidae)

Herons are the patient ones. We usually see them standing still as yard sculptures, waiting for a meal to swim within striking range. Herons come as small and secretive as the Least Bittern to as large and omnipresent as the tall, elegant Great Blue Heron. The group of lovely white birds we call egrets also belongs to the family of herons. Not all egrets are white; there is the Reddish Egret, which does produce a white morph, as does the Great Blue. And the immature Little Blue is as white as the Snowy Egret.

Least Bittern
Ixobrychus exilis

Date of Sighting

Location of Sighting

Notes

American Bittern
Botaurus lentiginosus

Date of Sighting

Location of Sighting

Notes

39

Black-crowned Night-Heron
Nycticorax nycticorax

Date of Sighting

Location of Sighting

Notes

Yellow-crowned Night-Heron
Nyctanassa violacea

Date of Sighting

Location of Sighting

Notes

Green Heron
Butorides virescens

Date of Sighting

Location of Sighting

Notes

Tricolored Heron
Egretta tricolor

Date of Sighting

Location of Sighting

Notes

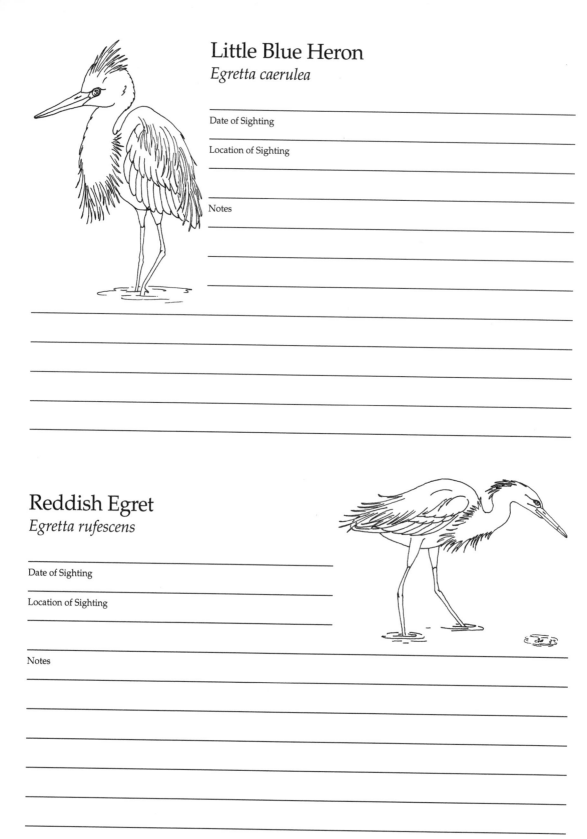

Little Blue Heron
Egretta caerulea

Date of Sighting

Location of Sighting

Notes

Reddish Egret
Egretta rufescens

Date of Sighting

Location of Sighting

Notes

Cattle Egret
Bubulcus ibis

Date of Sighting

Location of Sighting

Notes

Little Egret
Egretta garzetta

Date of Sighting

Location of Sighting

Notes

Snowy Egret
Egretta thula

Date of Sighting

Location of Sighting

Notes

Great Egret
Ardea alba

Date of Sighting

Location of Sighting

Notes

Great Blue Heron
Ardea herodias

Date of Sighting

Location of Sighting

Notes

Storks

(family Ciconiidae)

Storks impress us as being serious and deliberate. They have to be—our mythology has given them the extraordinary responsibility of delivering our babies safely and to the correct address.

Wood Stork

Mycteria americana

Date of Sighting

Location of Sighting

Notes

Jabiru

Jabiru mycteria

Date of Sighting

Location of Sighting

Notes

Flamingos
(family Phoenicopteridae)

I first saw flamingos in the wild on the island of Bonaire off the coast of Venezuela. In flight, they are improbable: long legs trailing behind, perfectly counterbalanced by an equally long neck projecting out front. They look like delicate pink kites keenly balanced on the breeze. You are most likely to see Greater Flamingoes in Florida Bay, in Everglades National Park, or along the Texas coast.

Greater Flamingo
Phoenicopterus ruber

Date of Sighting

Location of Sighting

Notes

Ibises and Spoonbills

(family Threskiornithidae)

It is curious that ibises and spoonbills, birds so different in appearance, are in the same family. But they occupy the same niche in nature, feeding on crustaceans in the shallows. The ibis probes deep into the mud with its long, decurved beak while the spoonbill sweeps its big, spatulate beak along the water surface, swirling up savory bits of food in its wake.

Glossy Ibis
Plegadis falcinellus

Date of Sighting

Location of Sighting

Notes

White-faced Ibis
Plegadis chihi

Date of Sighting

Location of Sighting

Notes

White Ibis
Eudocimus albus

Date of Sighting

Location of Sighting

Notes

Roseate Spoonbill
Ajaia ajaja

Date of Sighting

Location of Sighting

Notes

Swans, Geese, and Ducks

(family Anatidae)

There are four species of swans, nine species of geese, and over forty species of ducks we can see in North America. This great and varied family of birds has played a large part in American history. They have been hunted for food by every generation of man that has lived on this continent; working decoys of ducks exist from ancient civilizations, and hand-carved replicas today have been elevated to the realm of fine art. It was our modern duck hunters who led the way in conserving these migratory waterfowl by establishing national wildlife refuges. This marvelous system provides much-needed habitat for nongamebird species as well.

Tundra Swan
Cygnus columbianus

Date of Sighting

Location of Sighting

Notes

Trumpeter Swan
Cygnus buccinator

Date of Sighting

Location of Sighting

Notes

Whooper Swan
Cygnus cygnus

Date of Sighting

Location of Sighting

Notes

Mute Swan
Cygnus olor

Date of Sighting

Location of Sighting

Notes

Greater White-fronted Goose
Anser albifrons

Date of Sighting

Location of Sighting

Notes

Bean Goose
Anser fabalis

Date of Sighting

Location of Sighting

Notes

Pink-footed Goose
Anser brachyrhynchus

Date of Sighting

Location of Sighting

Notes

Snow Goose
Chen caerulescens

Date of Sighting

Location of Sighting

Notes

Ross's Goose
Chen rossii

Date of Sighting

Location of Sighting

Notes

Emperor Goose
Chen canagica

Date of Sighting

Location of Sighting

Notes

Canada Goose
Branta canadensis

Date of Sighting

Location of Sighting

Notes

Brant
Branta bernicla

Date of Sighting

Location of Sighting

Notes

Barnacle Goose
Branta leucopsis

Date of Sighting

Location of Sighting

Notes

Fulvous Whistling-Duck
Dendrocygna bicolor

Date of Sighting

Location of Sighting

Notes

Black-bellied Whistling-Duck
Dendrocygna autumnalis

Date of Sighting

Location of Sighting

Notes

Wood Duck
Aix sponsa

Date of Sighting

Location of Sighting

Notes

Muscovy Duck
Cairina moschata

Date of Sighting
_____

Location of Sighting
_____

_____

Notes
_____

_____

_____

_____

_____

_____

_____

_____

Mallard
Anas platyrhynchos

Date of Sighting
_____

Location of Sighting
_____

_____

Notes
_____

_____

_____

_____

_____

_____

_____

_____

Mottled Duck
Anas fulvigula

Date of Sighting

Location of Sighting

Notes

American Black Duck
Anas rubripes

Date of Sighting

Location of Sighting

Notes

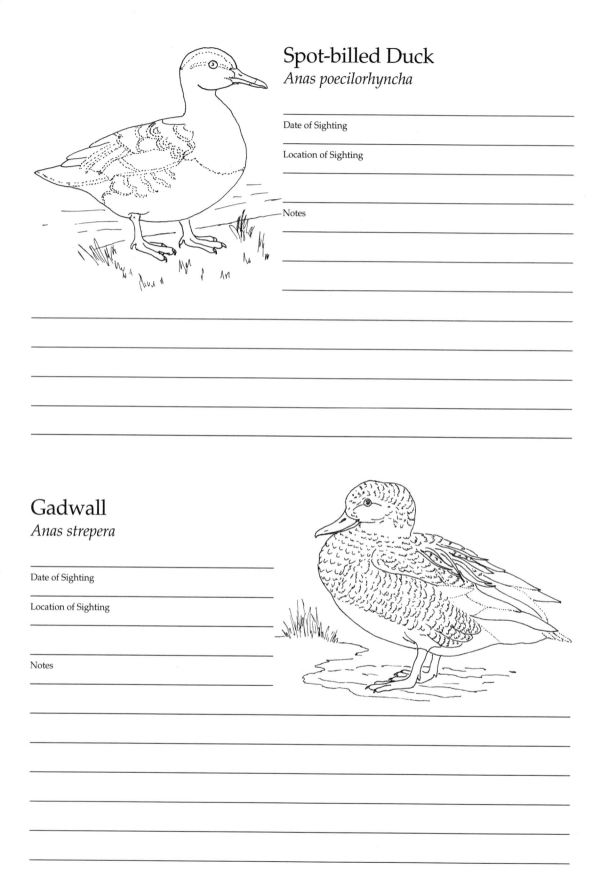

Spot-billed Duck
Anas poecilorhyncha

Date of Sighting

Location of Sighting

Notes

Gadwall
Anas strepera

Date of Sighting

Location of Sighting

Notes

Falcated Duck
Anas falcata

Date of Sighting

Location of Sighting

Notes

Green-winged Teal
Anas crecca

Date of Sighting

Location of Sighting

Notes

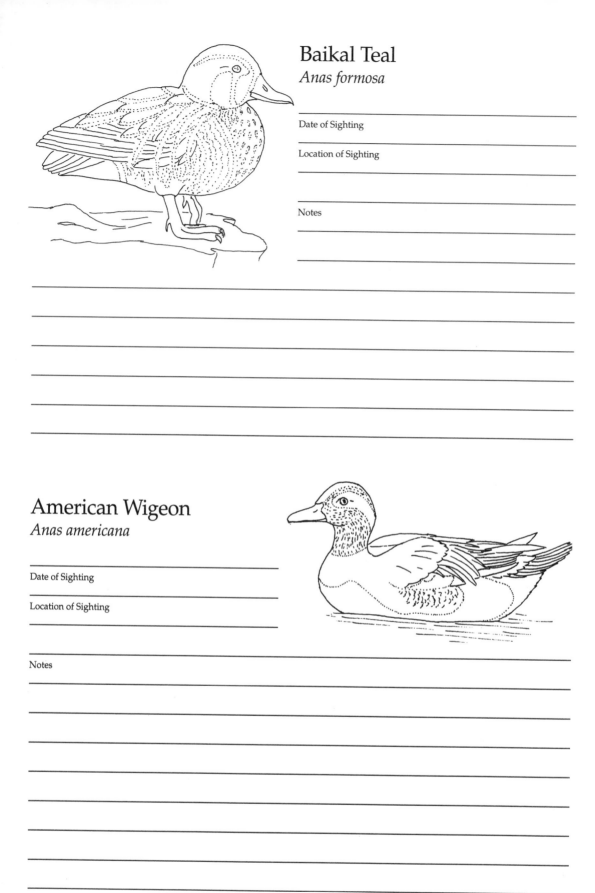

Baikal Teal
Anas formosa

Date of Sighting

Location of Sighting

Notes

American Wigeon
Anas americana

Date of Sighting

Location of Sighting

Notes

Eurasian Wigeon
Anas penelope

Date of Sighting

Location of Sighting

Notes

Northern Pintail
Anas acuta

Date of Sighting

Location of Sighting

Notes

White-cheeked Pintail
Anas bahamensis

Date of Sighting

Location of Sighting

Notes

Northern Shoveler
Anas clypeata

Date of Sighting

Location of Sighting

Notes

Blue-winged Teal
Anas discors

Date of Sighting

Location of Sighting

Notes

Gargany
Anas querquedula

Date of Sighting

Location of Sighting

Notes

Cinnamon Teal
Anas cyanoptera

Date of Sighting

Location of Sighting

Notes

Canvasback
Aythya valisineria

Date of Sighting

Location of Sighting

Notes

Common Pochard
Aythya ferina

Date of Sighting

Location of Sighting

Notes

Redhead
Aythya americana

Date of Sighting

Location of Sighting

Notes

Ring-necked Duck
Aythya collaris

Date of Sighting

Location of Sighting

Notes

Tufted Duck
Aythya fuligula

Date of Sighting

Location of Sighting

Notes

Greater Scaup
Aythya marila

Date of Sighting

Location of Sighting

Notes

Lesser Scaup
Aythya affinis

Date of Sighting

Location of Sighting

Notes

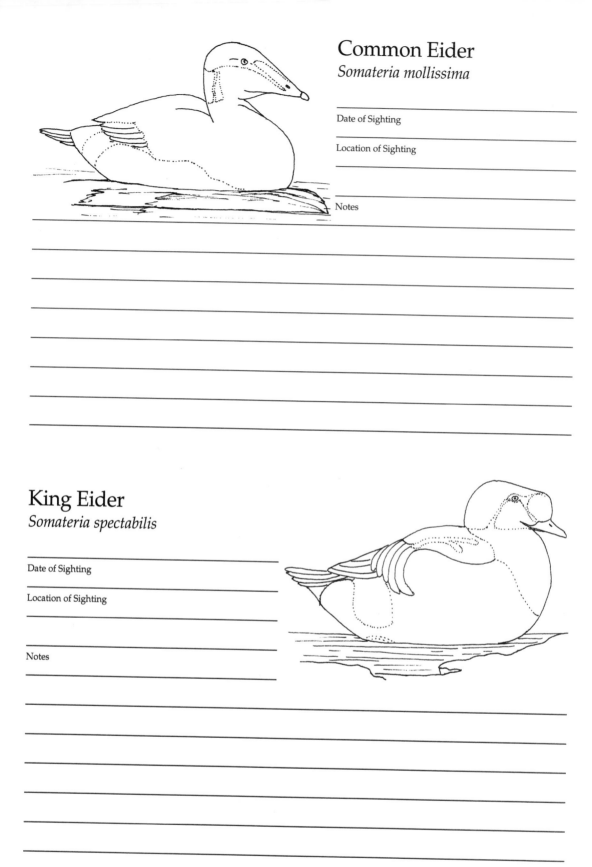

Common Eider
Somateria mollissima

Date of Sighting

Location of Sighting

Notes

King Eider
Somateria spectabilis

Date of Sighting

Location of Sighting

Notes

Spectacled Eider
Somateria fischeri

Date of Sighting

Location of Sighting

Notes

Steller's Eider
Polysticta stelleri

Date of Sighting

Location of Sighting

Notes

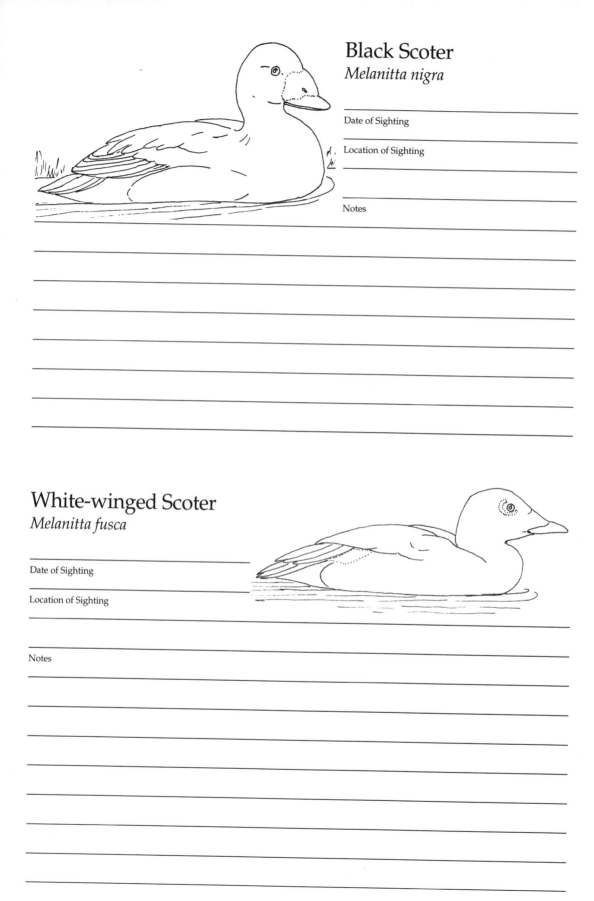

Black Scoter
Melanitta nigra

Date of Sighting

Location of Sighting

Notes

White-winged Scoter
Melanitta fusca

Date of Sighting

Location of Sighting

Notes

Surf Scoter
Melanitta perspicillata

Date of Sighting

Location of Sighting

Notes

Harlequin Duck
Histrionicus histrionicus

Date of Sighting

Location of Sighting

Notes

Long-tailed Duck
Clangula hyemalis

Date of Sighting

Location of Sighting

Notes

Barrow's Goldeneye
Bucephala islandica

Date of Sighting

Location of Sighting

Notes

Common Goldeneye
Bucephala clangula

Date of Sighting

Location of Sighting

Notes

Bufflehead
Bucephala albeola

Date of Sighting

Location of Sighting

Notes

Common Merganser
Mergus merganser

Date of Sighting

Location of Sighting

Notes

Red-breasted Merganser
Mergus serrator

Date of Sighting

Location of Sighting

Notes

Hooded Merganser
Lophodytes cucullatus

Date of Sighting

Location of Sighting

Notes

Smew
Mergellus albellus

Date of Sighting

Location of Sighting

Notes

Ruddy Duck
Oxyura jamaicensis

Date of Sighting

Location of Sighting

Notes

Masked Duck
Nomonyx dominicus

Date of Sighting

Location of Sighting

Notes

New World Vultures
(family Cathartidae)

We are fortunate to still have the California Condor with us. In 1987, the last few remaining wild birds were captured and placed in a captive-breeding program. Today, we have two populations successfully breeding in the wild: one in California and the other in Arizona. Recent studies indicate that New World vultures, which also include the Turkey and Black vultures, are more closely related to storks than they are to raptors, as previously believed.

Turkey Vulture
Cathartes aura

Date of Sighting

Location of Sighting

Notes

Black Vulture
Coragyps atratus

Date of Sighting

Location of Sighting

Notes

California Condor
Gymnogyps californianus

Date of Sighting

Location of Sighting

Notes

Kites, Eagles, and Hawks
(family Accipitridae)

The first time I saw a Swallow-tailed Kite I stared through my binoculars in disbelief. It was defying gravity, like a skein of silk lofting through the air buoyed by unseen winds. I knew little about birds at the time, but I was hooked by this moment, and instantly became a dedicated birder. All the members of this predaceous family are fine fliers, but none in my mind equals the elegance of the Swallow-tailed Kite.

Osprey
Pandion haliaetus

Date of Sighting

Location of Sighting

Notes

Mississippi Kite
Ictinia mississippiensis

Date of Sighting

Location of Sighting

Notes

Swallow-tailed Kite
Elanoides forficatus

Date of Sighting

Location of Sighting

Notes

White-tailed Kite
Elanus leucurus

Date of Sighting

Location of Sighting

Notes

Snail Kite
Rostrhamus sociabilis

Date of Sighting

Location of Sighting

Notes

Hook-billed Kite
Chondrohierax uncinatus

Date of Sighting

Location of Sighting

Notes

Northern Harrier
Circus cyaneus

Date of Sighting

Location of Sighting

Notes

Golden Eagle
Aquila chrysaetos

Date of Sighting

Location of Sighting

Notes

White-tailed Eagle
Haliaeetus albicilla

Date of Sighting

Location of Sighting

Notes

Steller's Sea-Eagle
Haliaeetus pelagicus

Date of Sighting

Location of Sighting

Notes

Bald Eagle
Haliaeetus leucocephalus

Date of Sighting

Location of Sighting

Notes

Sharp-shinned Hawk
Accipiter striatus

Date of Sighting

Location of Sighting

Notes

Cooper's Hawk
Accipiter cooperii

Date of Sighting

Location of Sighting

Notes

Northern Goshawk
Accipiter gentilis

Date of Sighting

Location of Sighting

Notes

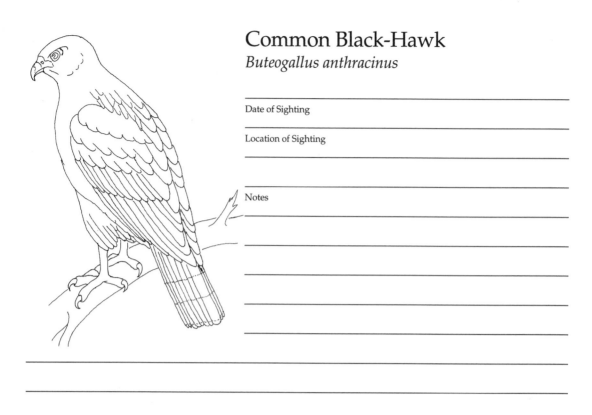

Common Black-Hawk
Buteogallus anthracinus

Date of Sighting

Location of Sighting

Notes

Harris's Hawk
Parabuteo unicinctus

Date of Sighting

Location of Sighting

Notes

Zone-tailed Hawk
Buteo albonotatus

Date of Sighting

Location of Sighting

Notes

Short-tailed Hawk
Buteo brachyurus

Date of Sighting

Location of Sighting

Notes

Broad-winged Hawk
Buteo platypterus

Date of Sighting

Location of Sighting

Notes

Gray Hawk
Asturina nitida

Date of Sighting

Location of Sighting

Notes

Red-shouldered Hawk
Buteo lineatus

Date of Sighting

Location of Sighting

Notes

Red-tailed Hawk
Buteo jamaicensis

Date of Sighting

Location of Sighting

Notes

Swainson's Hawk
Buteo swainsoni

Date of Sighting

Location of Sighting

Notes

Rough-legged Hawk
Buteo lagopus

Date of Sighting

Location of Sighting

Notes

Ferruginous Hawk
Buteo regalis

Date of Sighting

Location of Sighting

Notes

White-tailed Hawk
Buteo albicaudatus

Date of Sighting

Location of Sighting

Notes

Falcons and Caracaras
(family Falconidae)

The name "falcon" evokes an image of a fast, fierce predator—and the image is accurate. The Peregrine Falcon can reach speeds approaching two hundred miles per hour during its attack dive, known as a stoop. In addition to being swift and agile fliers, falcons are also extraordinarily lovely birds. Our smallest falcon, the American Kestrel, distributed throughout North America, is one of the most beautiful birds you will ever see.

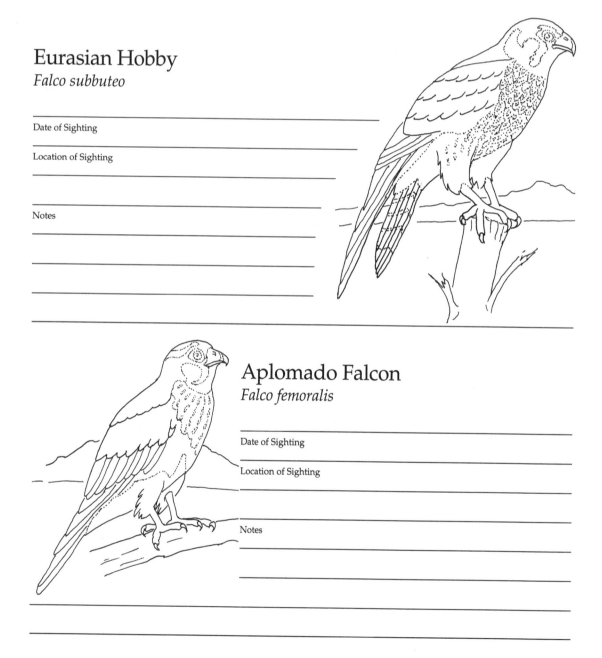

Eurasian Hobby
Falco subbuteo

Date of Sighting

Location of Sighting

Notes

Aplomado Falcon
Falco femoralis

Date of Sighting

Location of Sighting

Notes

Crested Caracara
Caracara plancus

Date of Sighting
_____

Location of Sighting
_____

_____

Notes
_____

_____

_____

_____

_____

_____

_____

_____

_____

_____

_____

American Kestrel
Falco sparverius

Date of Sighting
_____

Location of Sighting
_____

_____

Notes
_____

_____

_____

_____

_____

_____

_____

_____

_____

Eurasian Kestrel
Falco tinnunculus

Date of Sighting

Location of Sighting

Notes

Merlin
Falco columbarius

Date of Sighting

Location of Sighting

Notes

Prairie Falcon
Falco mexicanus

Date of Sighting
_____

Location of Sighting
_____

_____

Notes
_____

_____

_____

_____

_____

_____

_____

Peregrine Falcon
Falco peregrinus

Date of Sighting
_____

Location of Sighting
_____

_____

Notes
_____

_____

_____

_____

_____

_____

_____

Gyrfalcon
Falco rusticolus

Date of Sighting

Location of Sighting

Notes

Chachalacas

(family Cracidae)

The name "chachalaca" mimics the call of this chickenlike bird. In North America, you can most likely see the chachalaca in the Rio Grande Valley of Texas. In much of its range south of the border, the chachalaca is considered prime table fare, which, along with habitat loss, is putting pressure on its population.

Plain Chachalaca
Ortalis vetula

Date of Sighting

Location of Sighting

Notes

Partridges, Turkeys, and Grouse
(family Phasianidae)

A steadfast re-introduction program has resulted in an increase in the population of our largest gamebird, the Wild Turkey. You can now see this courtly bird almost nationwide, often travelling in small flocks along the margins of fields and woods.

Chukar
Alectoris chukar

Date of Sighting

Location of Sighting

Notes

Gray Partridge
Perdix perdix

Date of Sighting

Location of Sighting

Notes

Ring-necked Pheasant
Phasianus colchicus

Date of Sighting

Location of Sighting

Notes

Wild Turkey
Meleagris gallopavo

Date of Sighting

Location of Sighting

Notes

Himalayan Snowcock
Tetraogallus himalayensis

Date of Sighting

Location of Sighting

Notes

Ruffed Grouse
Bonasa umbellus

Date of Sighting

Location of Sighting

Notes

Spruce Grouse
Falcipennis canadensis

Date of Sighting
_____

Location of Sighting
_____

_____

Notes
_____

_____

_____

_____

_____

_____

_____

_____

_____

Blue Grouse
Dendragapus obscurus

Date of Sighting
_____

Location of Sighting
_____

Notes
_____

_____

_____

_____

_____

_____

_____

_____

White-tailed Ptarmigan
Lagopus leucurus

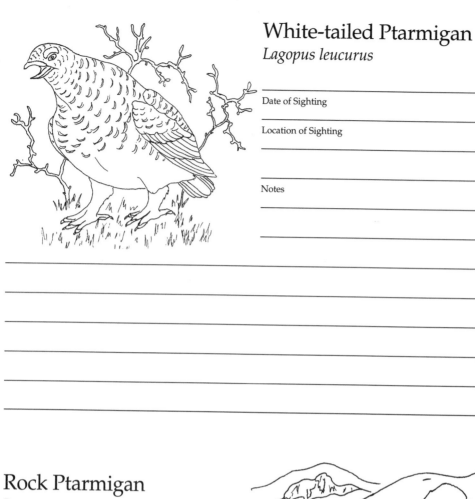

Date of Sighting

Location of Sighting

Notes

Rock Ptarmigan
Lagopus mutus

Date of Sighting

Location of Sighting

Notes

Willow Ptarmigan
Lagopus lagopus

Date of Sighting

Location of Sighting

Notes

Greater Prairie-Chicken
Tympanuchus cupido

Date of Sighting

Location of Sighting

Notes

Lesser Prairie-Chicken
Tympanuchus pallidicinctus

Date of Sighting

Location of Sighting

Notes

Sharp-tailed Grouse
Tympanuchus phasianellus

Date of Sighting

Location of Sighting

Notes

Greater Sage-Grouse
Centrocercus urophasianus

Date of Sighting

Location of Sighting

Notes

Gunnison Sage-Grouse
Centrocercus minimus

Date of Sighting

Location of Sighting

Notes

New World Quail
(family Odontophoridae)

Every species of this lovely family of ground dwellers makes succulent prey. In a balanced natural environment, a species can normally endure and adapt, even thrive, with heavy predation, but the quail population across the United States is in decline, due to habitat loss and to the predaceous impact of a rampant feral cat population.

Gambel's Quail
Callipepla gambelii

Date of Sighting

Location of Sighting

Notes

California Quail
Callipepla californica

Date of Sighting

Location of Sighting

Notes

Mountain Quail
Oreortyx pictus

Date of Sighting

Location of Sighting

Notes

Northern Bobwhite
Colinus virginianus

Date of Sighting

Location of Sighting

Notes

Montezuma Quail
Cyrtonyx montezumae

Date of Sighting

Location of Sighting

Notes

Scaled Quail
Callipepla squamata

Date of Sighting

Location of Sighting

Notes

Limpkins

(family Aramidae)

Over two feet long, this freshwater wader looks like a muscular rail. In fact, the solitary Limpkin has no close relatives. Preferring apple snails to all other foods, the Limpkin feeds in shallow freshwater swamps, marshes, and ponds, mainly in Florida.

Limpkin
Aramus guarauna

Date of Sighting

Location of Sighting

Notes

Rails, Gallinules, and Coots
(family Rallidae)

You are most likely to see gallinules and coots in the United States in the Southeast and along the Gulf Coast. But rails are a real challenge to bird-watchers, especially the Black Rail, a sparrow-size bird with the lungs of a barnyard rooster. I have heard the screaming call of this marsh denizen dozens of times, often only a few feet into the marsh, but I have never even glimpsed the secretive creature.

King Rail
Rallus elegans

Date of Sighting

Location of Sighting

Notes

Clapper Rail
Rallus longirostris

Date of Sighting

Location of Sighting

Notes

Virginia Rail
Rallus limicola

Date of Sighting

Location of Sighting

Notes

Sora
Porzana carolina

Date of Sighting

Location of Sighting

Notes

Yellow Rail
Coturnicops noveboracensis

Date of Sighting

Location of Sighting

Notes

Black Rail
Laterallus jamaicensis

Date of Sighting

Location of Sighting

Notes

Corn Crake
Crex crex

Date of Sighting

Location of Sighting

Notes

Purple Gallinule
Porphyrula martinica

Date of Sighting

Location of Sighting

Notes

Common Moorhen
Gallinula chloropus

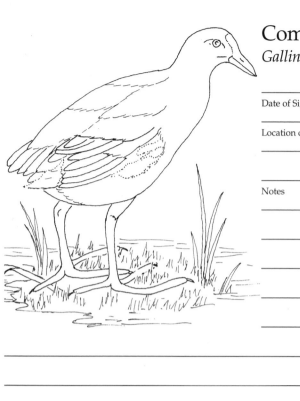

Date of Sighting

Location of Sighting

Notes

American Coot
Fulica americana

Date of Sighting

Location of Sighting

Notes

Eurasian Coot

Fulica atra

Date of Sighting

Location of Sighting

Notes

Cranes
(family Gruidae)

These tall long-legged birds are readily distinguished by the "bustle" of feathers covering their rumps. This decorative effect is actually created by the long tertial wing feathers that spill over the end of the bird when the wings are folded.

Sandhill Crane
Grus canadensis

Date of Sighting

Location of Sighting

Notes

Common Crane
Grus grus

Date of Sighting

Location of Sighting

Notes

Whooping Crane
Grus americana

Date of Sighting

Location of Sighting

Notes

Plovers and Lapwings
(family Charadriidae)

The Killdeer is probably the best-known plover in North America, famous for its broken wing display, as it attempts to lead intruders away from its ground nest. Plovers are ground feeders, usually running a few feet, stopping to feed, then running a few feet more. The general description of a plover is round-headed, large-eyed, short-billed, and long-legged. Through binoculars or a spotting scope, you can see that plovers are lovely, elegant birds.

Black-bellied Plover
Pluvialis squatarola

Date of Sighting

Location of Sighting

Notes

American Golden-Plover
Pluvialis dominica

Date of Sighting

Location of Sighting

Notes

Pacific Golden-Plover
Pluvialis fulva

Date of Sighting

Location of Sighting

Notes

European Golden-Plover
Pluvialis apricaria

Date of Sighting

Location of Sighting

Notes

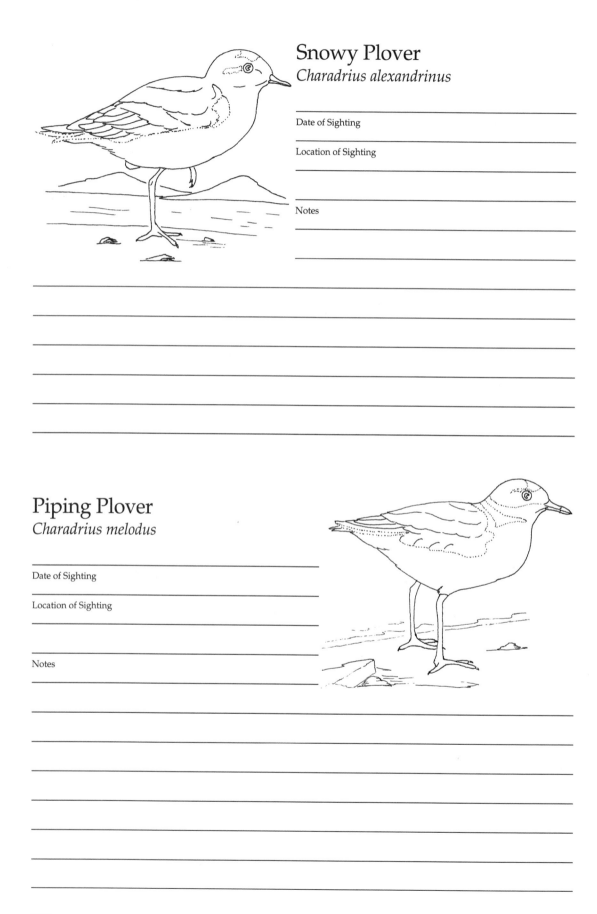

Snowy Plover
Charadrius alexandrinus

Date of Sighting

Location of Sighting

Notes

Piping Plover
Charadrius melodus

Date of Sighting

Location of Sighting

Notes

Wilson's Plover
Charadrius wilsonia

Date of Sighting

Location of Sighting

Notes

Semipalmated Plover
Charadrius semipalmatus

Date of Sighting

Location of Sighting

Notes

Common Ringed Plover
Charadrius hiaticula

Date of Sighting

Location of Sighting

Notes

Mongolian Plover
Charadrius mongolus

Date of Sighting

Location of Sighting

Notes

Little Ringed Plover
Charadrius dubius

Date of Sighting

Location of Sighting

Notes

Killdeer
Charadrius vociferus

Date of Sighting

Location of Sighting

Notes

Mountain Plover
Charadrius montanus

Date of Sighting

Location of Sighting

Notes

Northern Lapwing
Vanellus vanellus

Date of Sighting

Location of Sighting

Notes

Eurasian Dotterel
Charadrius morinellus

Date of Sighting

Location of Sighting

Notes

Jacanas
(family Jacanidae)

"Bigfoot" would be an appropriate name for this striking cinnamon and black shorebird with a bright yellow beak. Its feet are extremely long for its body, and the Northern Jacana uses them to walk on lily pads in search of food. The jacana visits Texas occasionally, and has even nested there.

Northern Jacana
Jacana spinosa

Date of Sighting

Location of Sighting

Notes

Oystercatchers

(family Haematopodidae)

The two species of oystercatchers in North America have long, stout, red bills that they use to quickly jab into slightly opened clams or oysters, cut the muscles, and eat the flesh.

Black Oystercatcher
Haematopus bachmani

Date of Sighting

Location of Sighting

Notes

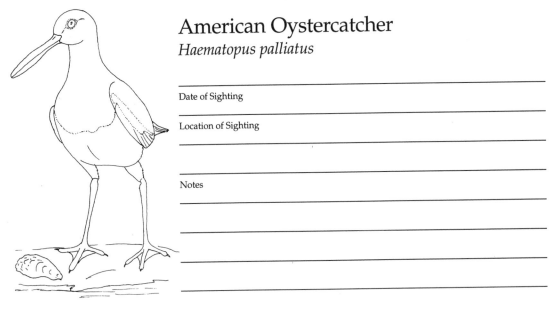

American Oystercatcher
Haematopus palliatus

Date of Sighting

Location of Sighting

Notes

Stilts and Avocets
(family Recurvirostridae)

We have one stilt and one avocet in North America, and both of these long-legged waders have strikingly elegant plumage. The Black-necked Stilt prefers to feed in the shallows of freshwater lakes and ponds; the American Avocet prefers a saltwater environment.

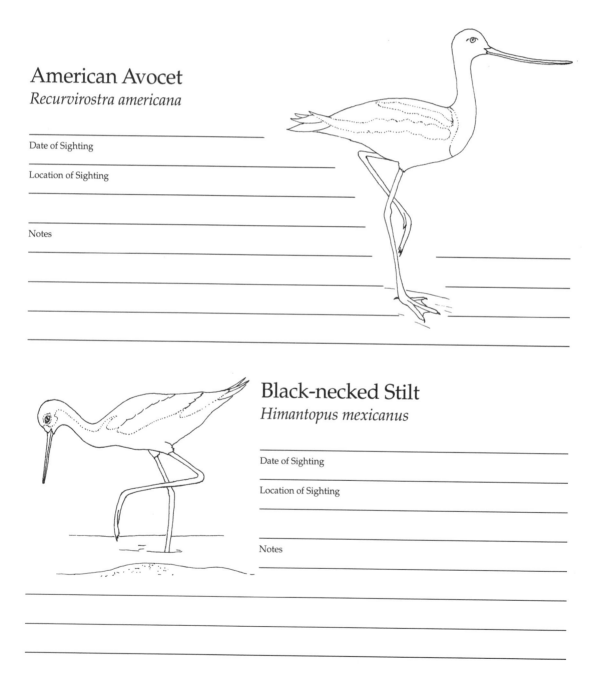

American Avocet
Recurvirostra americana

Date of Sighting

Location of Sighting

Notes

Black-necked Stilt
Himantopus mexicanus

Date of Sighting

Location of Sighting

Notes

Sandpipers and Phalaropes
(family Scolopacidae)

It is possible to see about sixty members of the sandpiper family in North America. They are generally found along the margins of oceans, lakes, and ponds; many are found inland as well. In fact, finding a sandpiper is not too difficult, but positively identifying it is one of birding's great challenges. The best ways to learn members of this varied and fascinating family are to go into the field with an expert, invest in a quality spotting scope, and spend time studying a good field guide. Plenty of field experience helps too.

Willet
Catoptrophorus semipalmatus

Date of Sighting

Location of Sighting

Notes

Greater Yellowlegs
Tringa melanoleuca

Date of Sighting

Location of Sighting

Notes

Lesser Yellowlegs
Tringa flavipes

Date of Sighting

Location of Sighting

Notes

Common Redshank
Tringa totanus

Date of Sighting

Location of Sighting

Notes

132

Common Greenshank
Tringa nebularia

Date of Sighting

Location of Sighting

Notes

Spotted Redshank
Tringa erythropus

Date of Sighting

Location of Sighting

Notes

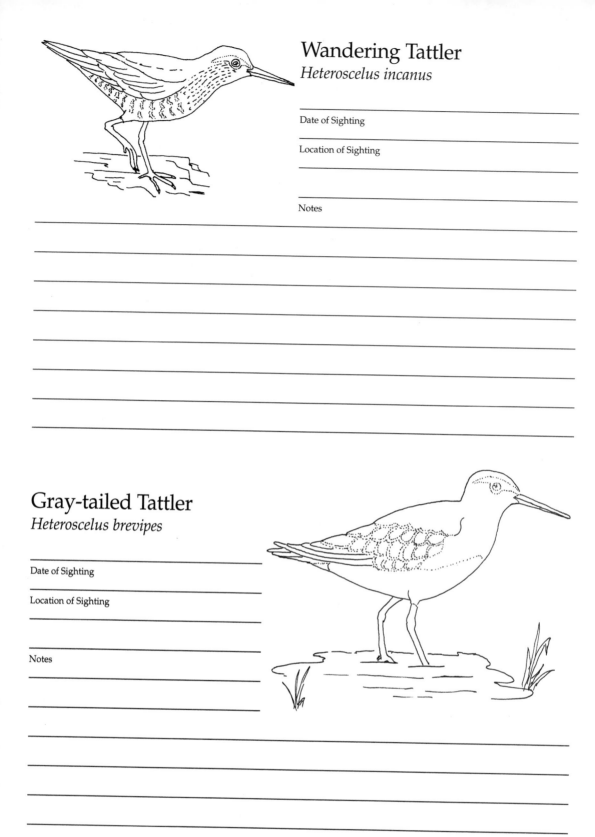

Wandering Tattler
Heteroscelus incanus

Date of Sighting

Location of Sighting

Notes

Gray-tailed Tattler
Heteroscelus brevipes

Date of Sighting

Location of Sighting

Notes

Green Sandpiper
Tringa ochropus

Date of Sighting

Location of Sighting

Notes

Wood Sandpiper
Tringa glareola

Date of Sighting

Location of Sighting

Notes

Solitary Sandpiper
Tringa solitaria

Date of Sighting

Location of Sighting

Notes

Spotted Sandpiper
Actitis macularia

Date of Sighting

Location of Sighting

Notes

Common Sandpiper
Actitis hypoleucos

Date of Sighting

Location of Sighting

Notes

Terek Sandpiper
Xenus cinereus

Date of Sighting

Location of Sighting

Notes

Eskimo Curlew
Numenius borealis

Date of Sighting

Location of Sighting

Notes

Whimbrel
Numenius phaeopus

Date of Sighting

Location of Sighting

Notes

Little Curlew
Numenius minutus

Date of Sighting

Location of Sighting

Notes

Bristle-thighed Curlew
Numenius tahitiensis

Date of Sighting

Location of Sighting

Notes

Long-billed Curlew
Numenius americanus

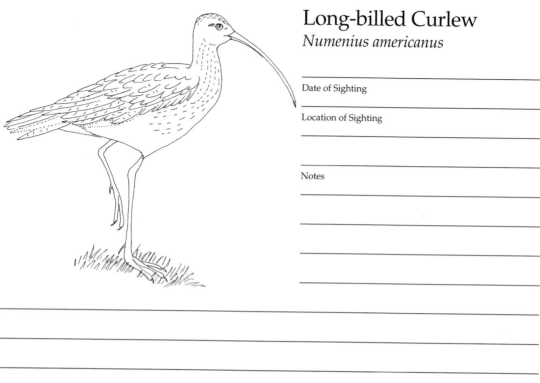

Date of Sighting

Location of Sighting

Notes

Far Eastern Curlew
Numenius madagascariensis

Date of Sighting

Location of Sighting

Notes

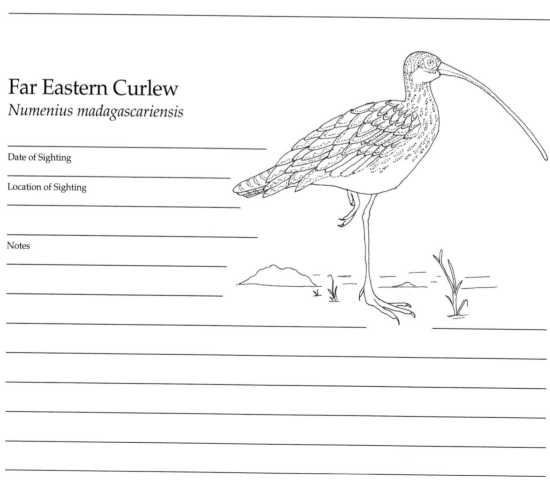

Eurasian Curlew
Numenius arquata

Date of Sighting

Location of Sighting

Notes

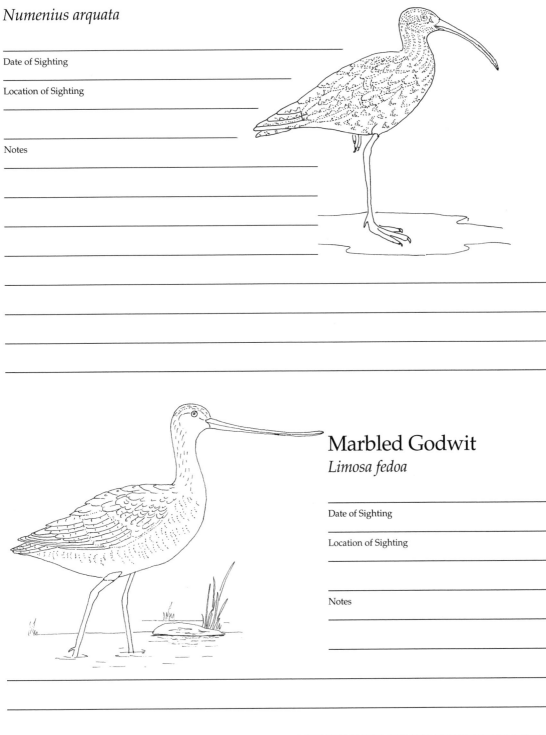

Marbled Godwit
Limosa fedoa

Date of Sighting

Location of Sighting

Notes

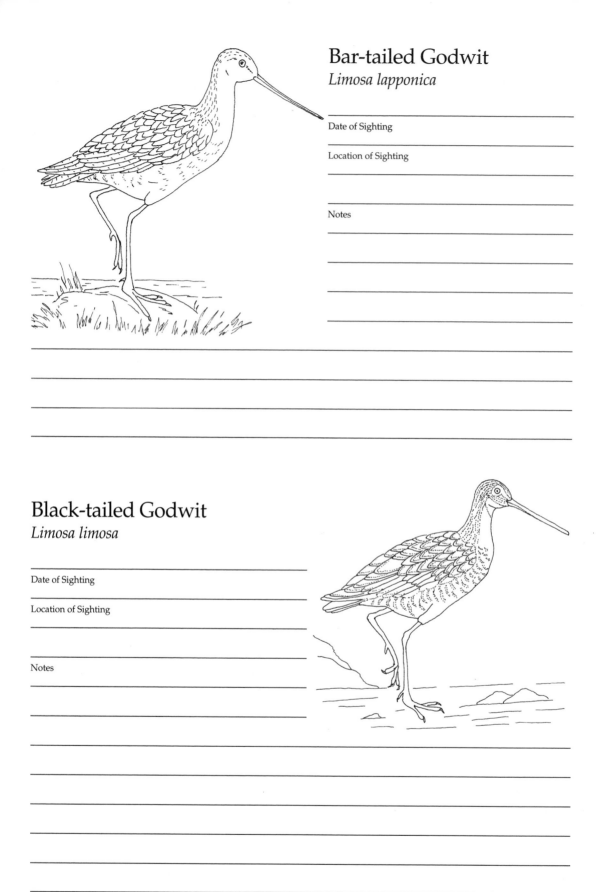

Bar-tailed Godwit
Limosa lapponica

Date of Sighting

Location of Sighting

Notes

Black-tailed Godwit
Limosa limosa

Date of Sighting

Location of Sighting

Notes

Hudsonian Godwit
Limosa haemastica

Date of Sighting

Location of Sighting

Notes

Ruddy Turnstone
Arenaria interpres

Date of Sighting

Location of Sighting

Notes

Black Turnstone
Arenaria melanocephala

Date of Sighting

Location of Sighting

Notes

Surfbird
Aphriza virgata

Date of Sighting

Location of Sighting

Notes

144

Rock Sandpiper
Calidris ptilocnemis

Date of Sighting

Location of Sighting

Notes

Purple Sandpiper
Calidris maritima

Date of Sighting

Location of Sighting

Notes

Great Knot
Calidris tenuirostris

Date of Sighting

Location of Sighting

Notes

Red Knot
Calidris canutus

Date of Sighting

Location of Sighting

Notes

Sanderling
Calidris alba

Date of Sighting

Location of Sighting

Notes

Dunlin
Calidris alpina

Date of Sighting

Location of Sighting

Notes

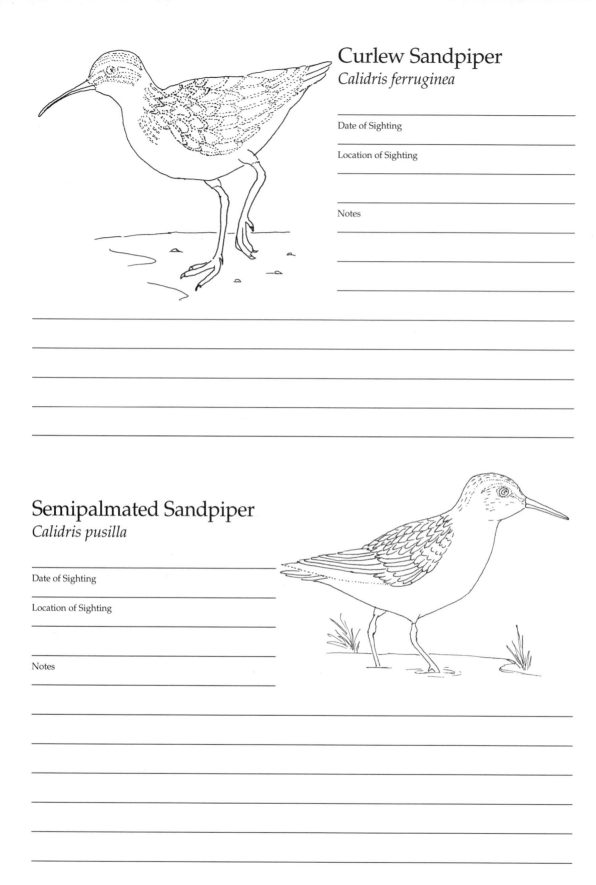

Curlew Sandpiper
Calidris ferruginea

Date of Sighting

Location of Sighting

Notes

Semipalmated Sandpiper
Calidris pusilla

Date of Sighting

Location of Sighting

Notes

Western Sandpiper
Calidris mauri

Date of Sighting

Location of Sighting

Notes

Least Sandpiper
Calidris minutilla

Date of Sighting

Location of Sighting

Notes

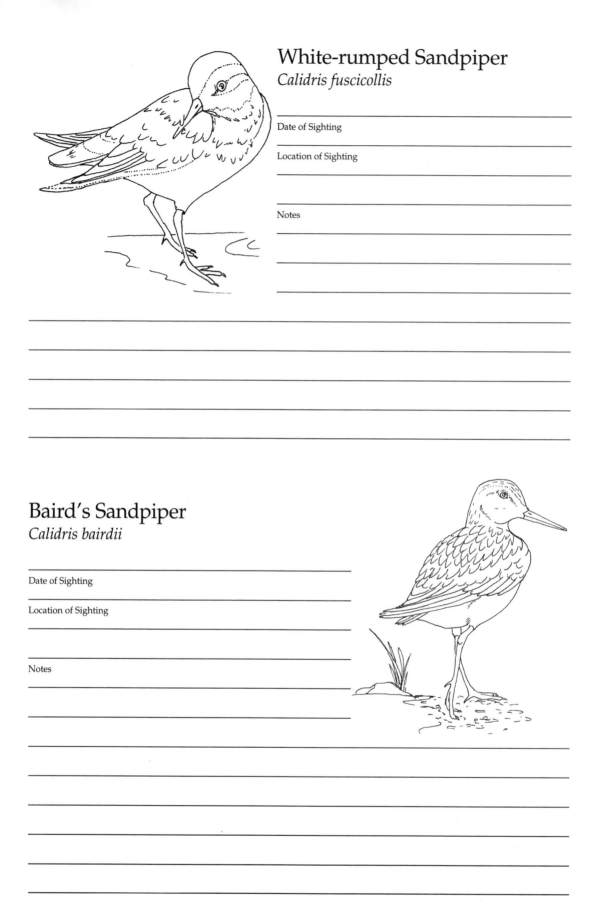

White-rumped Sandpiper
Calidris fuscicollis

Date of Sighting

Location of Sighting

Notes

Baird's Sandpiper
Calidris bairdii

Date of Sighting

Location of Sighting

Notes

Long-toed Stint
Calidris subminuta

Date of Sighting

Location of Sighting

Notes

Little Stint
Calidris minuta

Date of Sighting

Location of Sighting

Notes

Temminck's Stint
Calidris temminckii

Date of Sighting

Location of Sighting

Notes

Red-necked Stint
Calidris ruficollis

Date of Sighting

Location of Sighting

Notes

Spoonbill Sandpiper
Eurynorhynchus pygmeus

Date of Sighting

Location of Sighting

Notes

Broad-billed Sandpiper
Limicola falcinellus

Date of Sighting

Location of Sighting

Notes

Pectoral Sandpiper
Calidris melanotos

Date of Sighting

Location of Sighting

Notes

Sharp-tailed Sandpiper
Calidris acuminata

Date of Sighting

Location of Sighting

Notes

Upland Sandpiper
Bartramia longicauda

Date of Sighting

Location of Sighting

Notes

Buff-breasted Sandpiper
Tryngites subruficollis

Date of Sighting

Location of Sighting

Notes

Ruff
Philomachus pugnax

Date of Sighting

Location of Sighting

Notes

Short-billed Dowitcher
Limnodromus griseus

Date of Sighting

Location of Sighting

Notes

Long-billed Dowitcher
Limnodromus scolopaceus

Date of Sighting

Location of Sighting

Notes

Stilt Sandpiper
Calidris himantopus

Date of Sighting

Location of Sighting

Notes

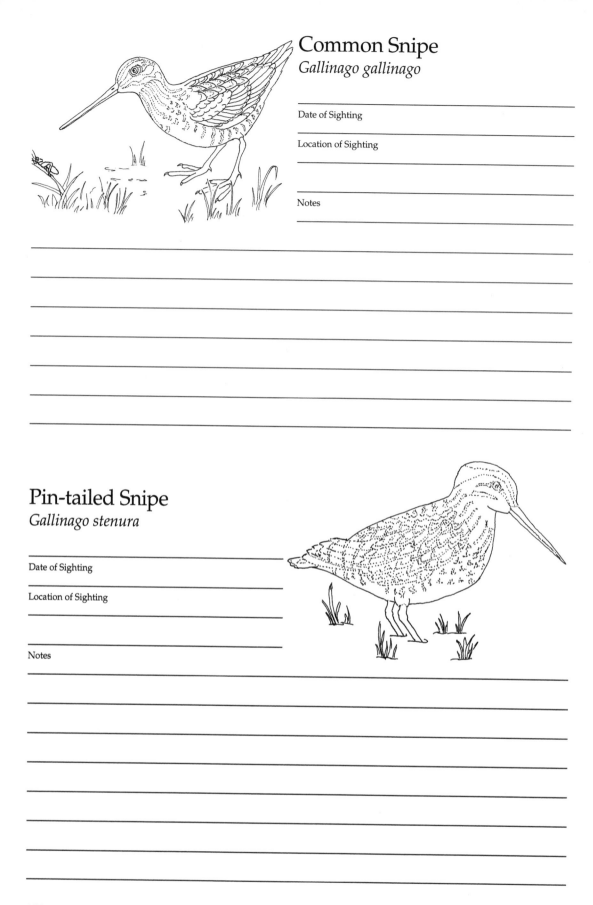

Common Snipe
Gallinago gallinago

Date of Sighting

Location of Sighting

Notes

Pin-tailed Snipe
Gallinago stenura

Date of Sighting

Location of Sighting

Notes

American Woodcock
Scolopax minor

Date of Sighting

Location of Sighting

Notes

Jack Snipe
Lymnocryptes minimus

Date of Sighting

Location of Sighting

Notes

Wilson's Phalarope
Phalaropus tricolor

Date of Sighting

Location of Sighting

Notes

Red-necked Phalarope
Phalaropus lobatus

Date of Sighting

Location of Sighting

Notes

160

Red Phalarope
Phalaropus fulicaria

Date of Sighting

Location of Sighting

Notes

Skuas, Gulls, Terns, and Skimmers
(family Laridae)

Many times I have been asked "what is your favorite bird?" I cannot answer the question because I have so many favorite birds, and my favorites change as my experience grows. Near the top of the list, however, is this large family of birds. I first saw the dashing Black Skimmer, with its long red beak, the only bird with a lower mandible longer than the upper, slicing the surface of a pond in Chincoteague National Wildlife Refuge. The skimmer glided effortlessly through and over a crowd of egrets, often missing them by only inches and eliciting grunts of irritation every time it buzzed by.

Great Skua
Catharacta skua

Date of Sighting

Location of Sighting

Notes

South Polar Skua
Catharacta maccormicki

Date of Sighting

Location of Sighting

Notes

Pomarine Jaeger
Stercorarius pomarinus

_____

Date of Sighting

_____

Location of Sighting

_____

_____

Notes

_____

_____

_____

_____

_____

_____

_____

_____

Parasitic Jaeger
Stercorarius parasiticus

_____

Date of Sighting

_____

Location of Sighting

_____

_____

Notes

_____

_____

_____

_____

_____

_____

_____

Long-tailed Jaeger
Stercorarius longicaudus

Date of Sighting

Location of Sighting

Notes

Heermann's Gull
Larus heermanni

Date of Sighting

Location of Sighting

Notes

Franklin's Gull
Larus pipixcan

Date of Sighting

Location of Sighting

Notes

Laughing Gull
Larus atricilla

Date of Sighting

Location of Sighting

Notes

Bonaparte's Gull
Larus philadelphia

Date of Sighting

Location of Sighting

Notes

Black-headed Gull
Larus ridibundus

Date of Sighting

Location of Sighting

Notes

Little Gull
Larus minutus

Date of Sighting

Location of Sighting

Notes

Ross's Gull
Rhodostethia rosea

Date of Sighting

Location of Sighting

Notes

Ring-billed Gull
Larus delawarensis

Date of Sighting

Location of Sighting

Notes

Mew Gull
Larus canus

Date of Sighting

Location of Sighting

Notes

California Gull
Larus californicus

Date of Sighting

Location of Sighting

Notes

Black-tailed Gull
Larus crassirostris

Date of Sighting

Location of Sighting

Notes

Band-tailed Gull
Larus belcheri

Date of Sighting

Location of Sighting

Notes

Kelp Gull
Larus dominicanus

Date of Sighting

Location of Sighting

Notes

Herring Gull
Larus argentatus

Date of Sighting

Location of Sighting

Notes

Yellow-legged Gull
Larus cachinnans

Date of Sighting

Location of Sighting

Notes

Glaucous Gull
Larus hyperboreus

Date of Sighting

Location of Sighting

Notes

Iceland Gull
Larus glaucoides

Date of Sighting

Location of Sighting

Notes

Thayer's Gull
Larus thayeri

Date of Sighting

Location of Sighting

Notes

Yellow-footed Gull
Larus livens

Date of Sighting

Location of Sighting

Notes

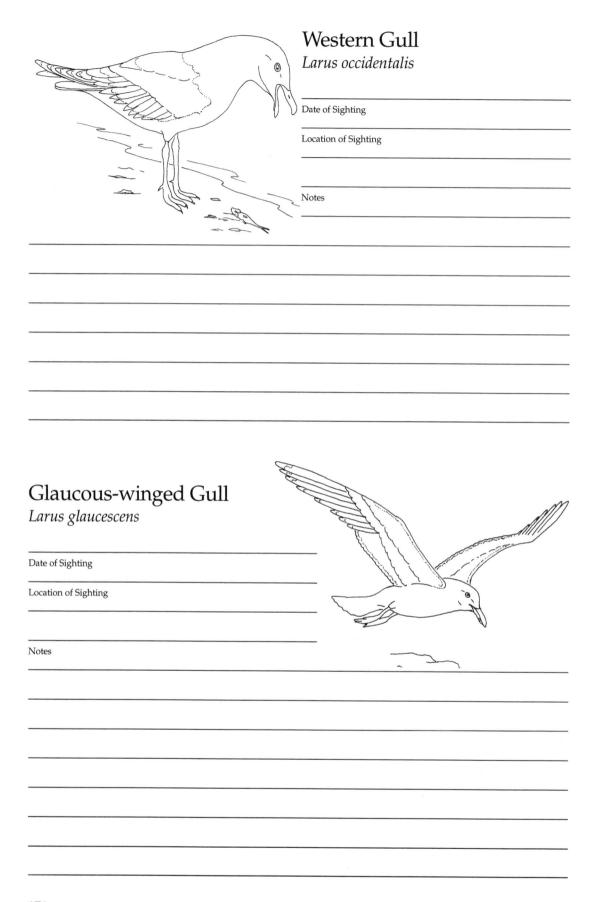

Western Gull
Larus occidentalis

Date of Sighting

Location of Sighting

Notes

Glaucous-winged Gull
Larus glaucescens

Date of Sighting

Location of Sighting

Notes

Slaty-backed Gull
Larus schistisagus

Date of Sighting

Location of Sighting

Notes

Lesser Black-backed Gull
Larus fuscus

Date of Sighting

Location of Sighting

Notes

Great Black-backed Gull
Larus marinus

Date of Sighting

Location of Sighting

Notes

Black-legged Kittiwake
Rissa tridactyla

Date of Sighting

Location of Sighting

Notes

Red-legged Kittiwake
Rissa brevirostris

Date of Sighting

Location of Sighting

Notes

Sabine's Gull
Xema sabini

Date of Sighting

Location of Sighting

Notes

Ivory Gull
Pagophila eburnea

Date of Sighting

Location of Sighting

Notes

Sandwich Tern
Sterna sandvicensis

Date of Sighting

Location of Sighting

Notes

Elegant Tern
Sterna elegans

Date of Sighting

Location of Sighting

Notes

Royal Tern
Sterna maxima

Date of Sighting

Location of Sighting

Notes

Caspian Tern
Sterna caspia

Date of Sighting

Location of Sighting

Notes

Roseate Tern
Sterna dougallii

Date of Sighting

Location of Sighting

Notes

Forster's Tern
Sterna forsteri

Date of Sighting

Location of Sighting

Notes

Gull-billed Tern
Sterna nilotica

Date of Sighting

Location of Sighting

Notes

Common Tern
Sterna hirundo

Date of Sighting

Location of Sighting

Notes

Arctic Tern
Sterna paradisaea

Date of Sighting

Location of Sighting

Notes

Aleutian Tern
Sterna aleutica

Date of Sighting

Location of Sighting

Notes

Least Tern
Sterna antillarum

Date of Sighting

Location of Sighting

Notes

Black Tern
Chlidonias niger

Date of Sighting

Location of Sighting

Notes

White-winged Tern
Chlidonias leucopterus

Date of Sighting

Location of Sighting

Notes

Bridled Tern
Sterna anaethetus

Date of Sighting

Location of Sighting

Notes

Sooty Tern
Sterna fuscata

Date of Sighting

Location of Sighting

Notes

Black Noddy
Anous minutus

Date of Sighting

Location of Sighting

Notes

Brown Noddy
Anous stolidus

Date of Sighting

Location of Sighting

Notes

Large-billed Tern
Phaetusa simplex

Date of Sighting

Location of Sighting

Notes

Black Skimmer
Rynchops niger

Date of Sighting

Location of Sighting

Notes

Murres, Auks, and Puffins
(family Alcidae)

Although they can fly, auks, murres, and puffins are, like penguins, excellent swimmers. I have watched Atlantic Puffins struggle from the water's surface to become airborne, then fly like short-winged bricks to their perches nearby. But in the water, these little "bricks" employ those same stubby wings as fins to swim with the grace and purpose of sharks. They feed on fish and mollusks, diving down two hundred feet.

Dovekie
Alle alle

_____
Date of Sighting

_____
Location of Sighting

_____

Notes
_____
_____
_____
_____

Common Murre
Uria aalge

_____
Date of Sighting

_____
Location of Sighting

_____

Notes
_____
_____

Thick-billed Murre
Uria lomvia

Date of Sighting

Location of Sighting

Notes

Razorbill
Alca torda

Date of Sighting

Location of Sighting

Notes

Black Guillemot
Cepphus grylle

Date of Sighting

Location of Sighting

Notes

Pigeon Guillemot
Cepphus columba

Date of Sighting

Location of Sighting

Notes

Long-billed Murrelet
Brachyramphus perdix

Date of Sighting

Location of Sighting

Notes

Marbled Murrelet
Brachyramphus marmoratus

Date of Sighting

Location of Sighting

Notes

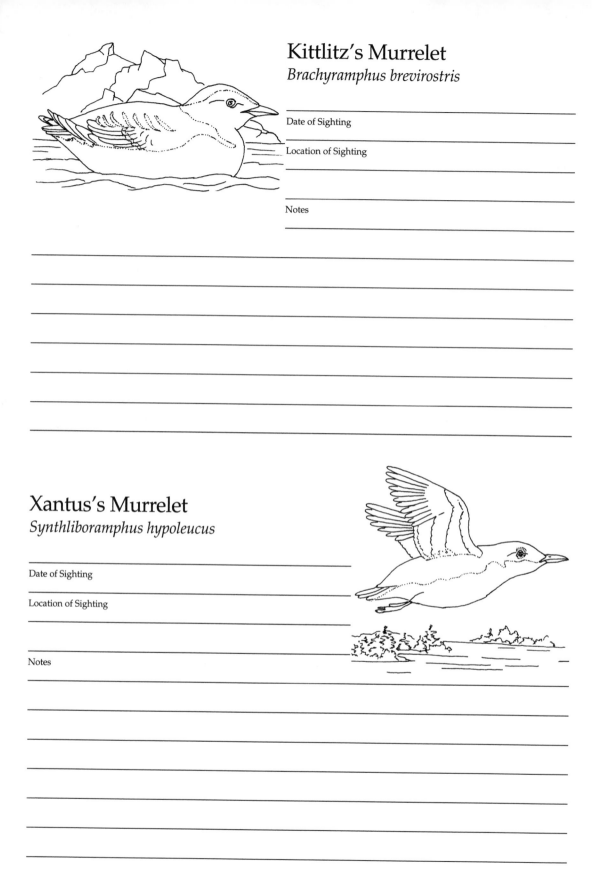

Kittlitz's Murrelet
Brachyramphus brevirostris

Date of Sighting

Location of Sighting

Notes

Xantus's Murrelet
Synthliboramphus hypoleucus

Date of Sighting

Location of Sighting

Notes

Craveri's Murrelet
Synthliboramphus craveri

Date of Sighting

Location of Sighting

Notes

Ancient Murrelet
Synthliboramphus antiquus

Date of Sighting

Location of Sighting

Notes

Cassin's Auklet
Ptychoramphus aleuticus

Date of Sighting

Location of Sighting

Notes

Parakeet Auklet
Aethia psittacula

Date of Sighting

Location of Sighting

Notes

Crested Auklet
Aethia cristatella

Date of Sighting

Location of Sighting

Notes

Whiskered Auklet
Aethia pygmaea

Date of Sighting

Location of Sighting

Notes

Least Auklet
Aethia pusilla

Date of Sighting

Location of Sighting

Notes

Rhinoceros Auklet
Cerorhinca monocerata

Date of Sighting

Location of Sighting

Notes

Atlantic Puffin
Fratercula arctica

Date of Sighting

Location of Sighting

Notes

Horned Puffin
Fratercula corniculata

Date of Sighting

Location of Sighting

Notes

Tufted Puffin
Fratercula cirrhata

Date of Sighting

Location of Sighting

Notes

Pigeons and Doves
(family Columbidae)

Pigeon milk is one of the most intriguing attributes of this family of birds. Both male and female pigeons and doves generate a fat- and protein-rich substance in their crops, which the young are fed almost exclusively for the first two weeks of their lives. The most common member of this family is the Rock Dove. Originally native to North Africa and India, the Rock Dove is the common "pigeon" now abundant in almost every city in the world.

Band-tailed Pigeon
Columba fasciata

Date of Sighting

Location of Sighting

Notes

Red-billed Pigeon
Columba flavirostris

Date of Sighting

Location of Sighting

Notes

White-crowned Pigeon
Columba leucocephala

Date of Sighting

Location of Sighting

Notes

Rock Dove
Columba livia

Date of Sighting

Location of Sighting

Notes

Zenaida Dove
Zenaida aurita

Date of Sighting

Location of Sighting

Notes

Mourning Dove
Zenaida macroura

Date of Sighting

Location of Sighting

Notes

Spotted Dove
Streptopelia chinensis

Date of Sighting

Location of Sighting

Notes

Eurasian Collared-Dove
Streptopelia decaocto

Date of Sighting

Location of Sighting

Notes

White-winged Dove
Zenaida asiatica

Date of Sighting

Location of Sighting

Notes

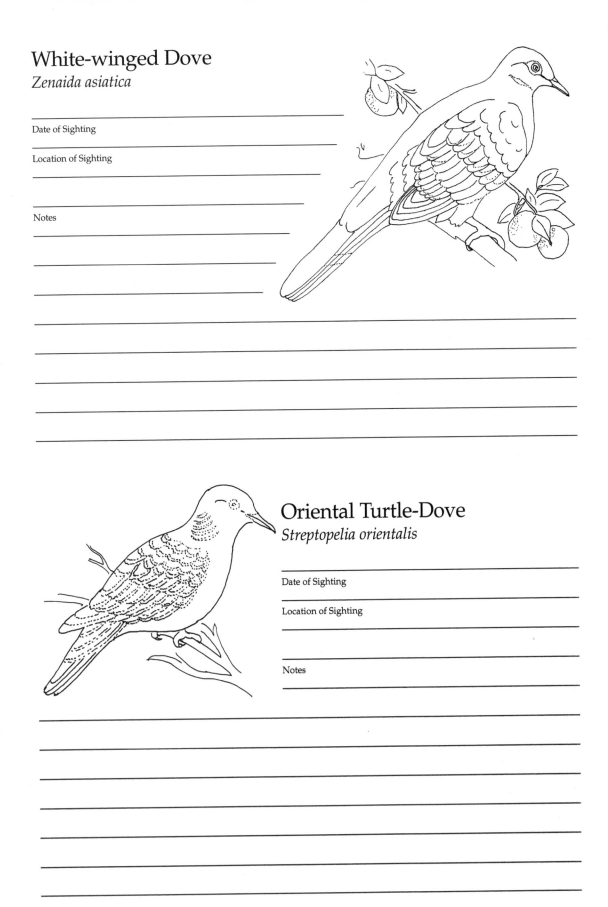

Oriental Turtle-Dove
Streptopelia orientalis

Date of Sighting

Location of Sighting

Notes

Common Ground-Dove
Columbina passerina

Date of Sighting

Location of Sighting

Notes

Ruddy Ground-Dove
Columbina talpacoti

Date of Sighting

Location of Sighting

Notes

Inca Dove
Columbina inca

Date of Sighting

Location of Sighting

Notes

White-tipped Dove
Leptotila verreauxi

Date of Sighting

Location of Sighting

Notes

Key West Quail-Dove
Geotrygon chrysia

Date of Sighting

Location of Sighting

Notes

Ruddy Quail-Dove
Geotrygon montana

Date of Sighting

Location of Sighting

Notes

Parakeets and Parrots

(family Psittacidae)

Since the loss of the Carolina Parakeet in the early 1900s there are no longer any native parrots living in North America. But we do have several breeding populations of escaped cage birds. One of the more notable is the Monk Parakeet. Colonies of this boisterous bird have been established throughout much of Florida, and the bird has moved into Delaware, Chicago, and Brooklyn. There is no telling where the monk may show up next.

White-winged Parakeet
Brotogeris versicolurus

Date of Sighting

Location of Sighting

Notes

Yellow-chevroned Parakeet
Brotogeris chiriri

Date of Sighting

Location of Sighting

Notes

Monk Parakeet
Myiopsitta monachus

Date of Sighting

Location of Sighting

Notes

Dusky-headed Parakeet
Aratinga weddelli

Date of Sighting

Location of Sighting

Notes

Black-hooded Parakeet
Nandayus nenday

Date of Sighting

Location of Sighting

Notes

Green Parakeet
Aratinga holochlora

Date of Sighting

Location of Sighting

Notes

Blue-crowned Parakeet
Aratinga acuticaudata

Date of Sighting

Location of Sighting

Notes

Mitred Parakeet
Aratinga mitrata

Date of Sighting

Location of Sighting

Notes

Red-masked Parakeet
Aratinga erythrogenys

Date of Sighting

Location of Sighting

Notes

Thick-billed Parrot
Rhynchopsitta pachyrhyncha

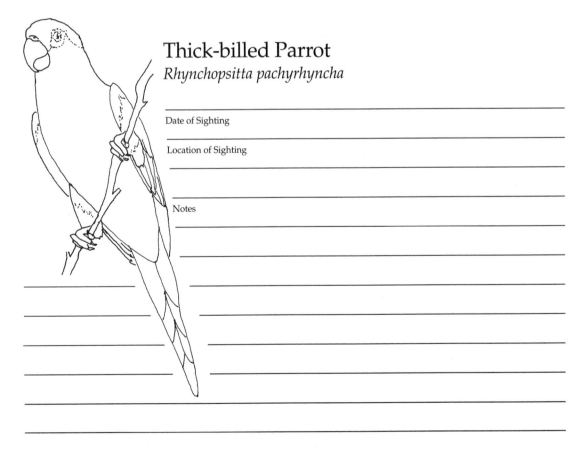

Date of Sighting

Location of Sighting

Notes

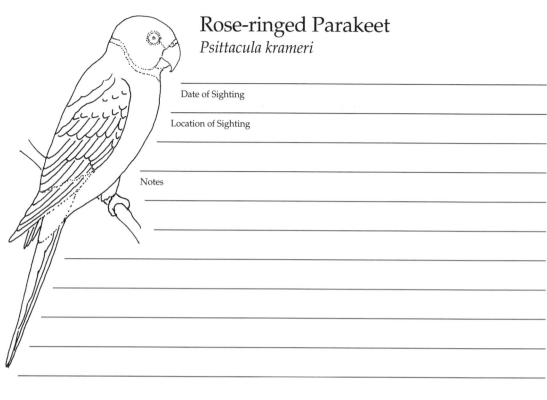

Rose-ringed Parakeet
Psittacula krameri

Date of Sighting

Location of Sighting

Notes

Red-crowned Parrot
Amazona viridigenalis

Date of Sighting

Location of Sighting

Notes

Orange-winged Parrot
Amazona amazonica

Date of Sighting

Location of Sighting

Notes

Lilac-crowned Parrot
Amazona finschi

Date of Sighting

Location of Sighting

Notes

Yellow-headed Parrot
Amazona oratrix

Date of Sighting

Location of Sighting

Notes

Budgerigar
Melopsittacus undulatus

Date of Sighting

Location of Sighting

Notes

Cuckoos, Roadrunners, and Anis
(family Cuculidae)

Both Black-billed and Yellow-billed Cuckoos eat the big, hairy caterpillars most other birds avoid. These are furtive, secretive birds more often heard than seen. The most famous cuckoo is the Greater Roadrunner, speeding along at fifteen-plus miles per hour in pursuit of lizards and insects. As a kid I spent hours watching these big birds racing through the New Mexican desert, sporting their distinctive long tail and a swoosh of bright blue behind their eyes. I still think they run for fun.

Mangrove Cuckoo
Coccyzus minor

Date of Sighting

Location of Sighting

Notes

Yellow-billed Cuckoo
Coccyzus americanus

Date of Sighting

Location of Sighting

Notes

Black-billed Cuckoo
Coccyzus erythropthalmus

Date of Sighting

Location of Sighting

Notes

Greater Roadrunner
Geococcyx californianus

Date of Sighting

Location of Sighting

Notes

Common Cuckoo
Cuculus canorus

Date of Sighting

Location of Sighting

Notes

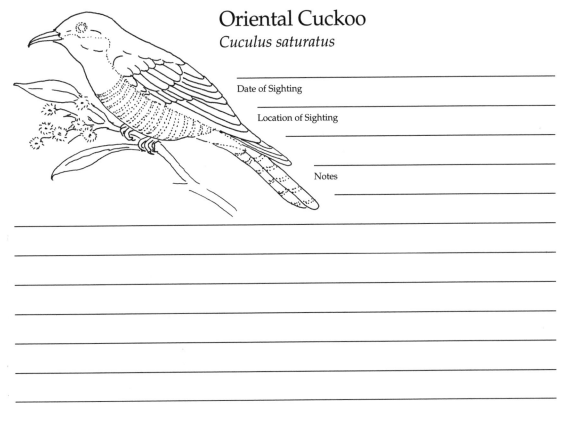

Oriental Cuckoo
Cuculus saturatus

Date of Sighting

Location of Sighting

Notes

Smooth-billed Ani
Crotophaga ani

Date of Sighting

Location of Sighting

Notes

Groove-billed Ani
Crotophaga sulcirostris

Date of Sighting

Location of Sighting

Notes

Owls

(families Tytonidae and Strigidae)

The common perception of the "wise old owl" may be more fiction than fact, but owls are undeniably among the most accomplished avian predators. Great Horned Owls are known to prey upon hawks and even the speedy Peregrine Falcon. When I saw my first Great Horned Owl I was stunned by the imposing size of the bird, which exuded the calm composure of a creature at the top of the food chain. Owls are generally night birds. The surest way to get to know owls is to get to know their calls.

Barn Owl
Tyto alba

Date of Sighting

Location of Sighting

Notes

Short-eared Owl
Asio flammeus

Date of Sighting

Location of Sighting

Notes

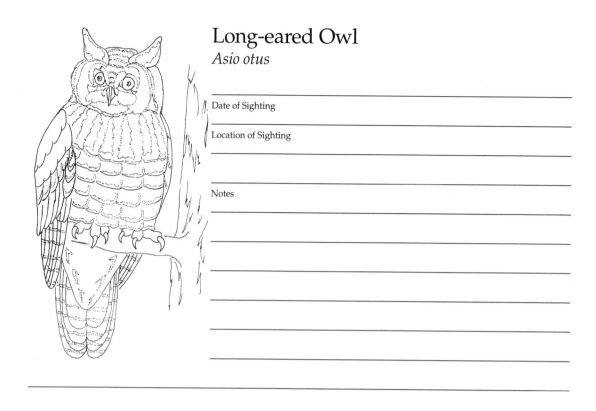

Long-eared Owl
Asio otus

Date of Sighting

Location of Sighting

Notes

Great Horned Owl
Bubo virginianus

Date of Sighting

Location of Sighting

Notes

Barred Owl
Strix varia

Date of Sighting

Location of Sighting

Notes

Great Gray Owl
Strix nebulosa

Date of Sighting

Location of Sighting

Notes

Spotted Owl
Strix occidentalis

Date of Sighting

Location of Sighting

Notes

Snowy Owl
Nyctea scandiaca

Date of Sighting

Location of Sighting

Notes

Eastern Screech-Owl
Otus asio

Date of Sighting

Location of Sighting

Notes

Western Screech-Owl
Otus kennicottii

Date of Sighting

Location of Sighting

Notes

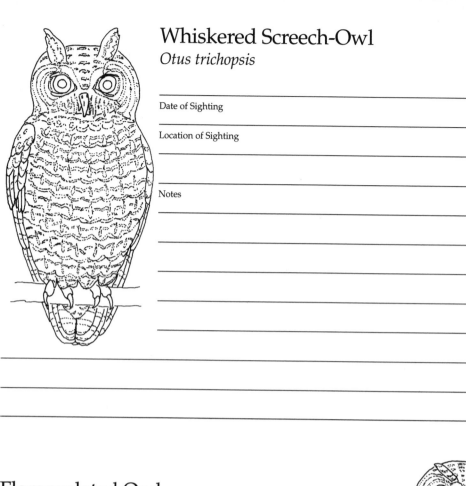

Whiskered Screech-Owl
Otus trichopsis

Date of Sighting

Location of Sighting

Notes

Flammulated Owl
Otus flammeolus

Date of Sighting

Location of Sighting

Notes

224

Ferruginous Pygmy-Owl
Glaucidium brasilianum

Date of Sighting

Location of Sighting

Notes

Elf Owl
Micrathene whitneyi

Date of Sighting

Location of Sighting

Notes

Northern Pygmy-Owl
Glaucidium gnoma

Date of Sighting

Location of Sighting

Notes

Northern Saw-whet Owl
Aegolius acadicus

Date of Sighting

Location of Sighting

Notes

Northern Hawk Owl
Surnia ulula

Date of Sighting

Location of Sighting

Notes

Boreal Owl
Aegolius funereus

Date of Sighting

Location of Sighting

Notes

Burrowing Owl
Athene cunicularia

Date of Sighting

Location of Sighting

Notes

Nighthawks and Nightjars
(family Caprimulgidae)

Have you ever felt a cold gust of wind hit the back of your neck? The call of the Whip-poor-will has the same chilling effect. The sound is otherworldly and unforgettable. This family of nocturnal birds is made up of extraordinary fliers. I was birding a small pine woods in central Florida late one spring afternoon when I heard a sound that almost made me jump out of my skin. It was a loud rattling sound, like someone dragging a stick along a picket fence. It was a Common Nighthawk performing its display flight. I stood transfixed while watching this incredible performance, one of my most memorable birding experiences.

Lesser Nighthawk
Chordeiles acutipennis

Date of Sighting

Location of Sighting

Notes

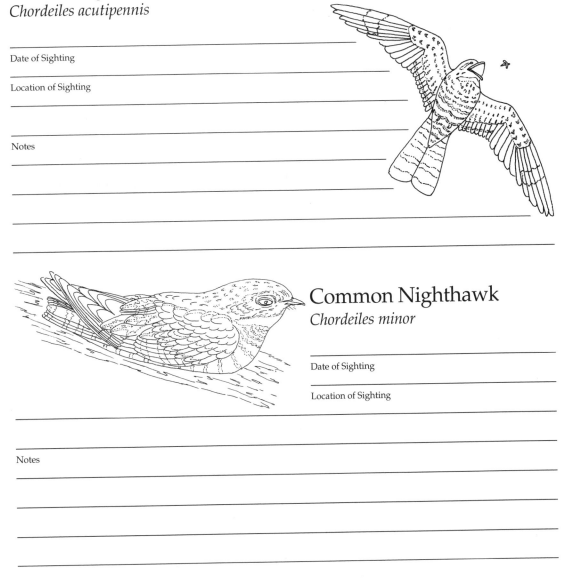

Common Nighthawk
Chordeiles minor

Date of Sighting

Location of Sighting

Notes

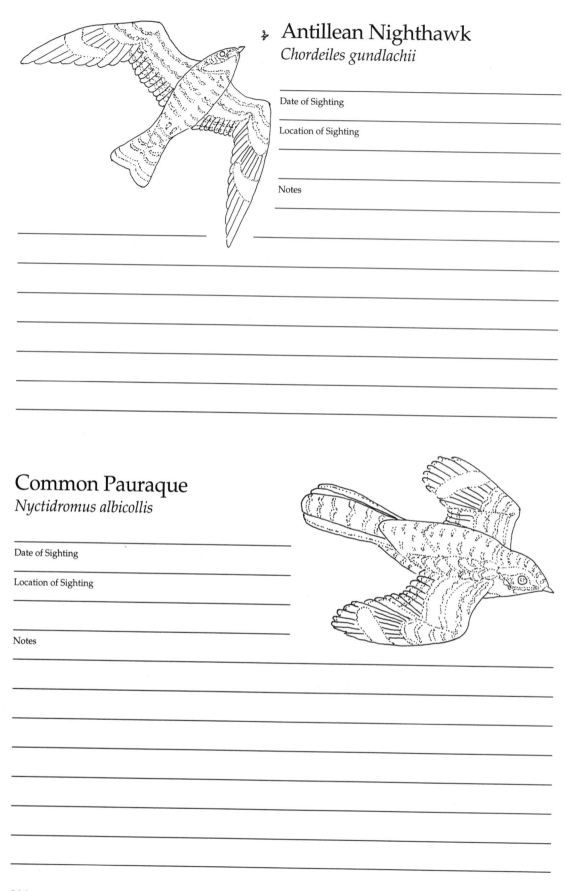

Antillean Nighthawk
Chordeiles gundlachii

Date of Sighting

Location of Sighting

Notes

Common Pauraque
Nyctidromus albicollis

Date of Sighting

Location of Sighting

Notes

Chuck-will's-widow
Caprimulgus carolinensis

Date of Sighting

Location of Sighting

Notes

Whip-poor-will
Caprimulgus vociferus

Date of Sighting

Location of Sighting

Notes

Buff-collared Nightjar
Caprimulgus ridgwayi

Date of Sighting

Location of Sighting

Notes

Common Poorwill
Phalaenoptilus nuttallii

Date of Sighting

Location of Sighting

Notes

Swifts

(family Apodidae)

Swifts are indeed swift and they seem to love to fly. Some swifts are such accomplished fliers it is believed they even sleep on the wing. Our most common North American swift, the Chimney Swift, gathers nesting material by snapping off small dead twigs during fly-bys. True to its name, the Chimney Swift builds its muddy nest on the inside of chimney walls, raising four to five young each year. Often described as a cigar with wings, the Chimney Swift can be seen flying high in the air during the evening gathering insects on the wing.

Black Swift
Cypseloides niger

Date of Sighting

Location of Sighting

Notes

Vaux's Swift
Chaetura vauxi

Date of Sighting

Location of Sighting

Notes

Chimney Swift
Chaetura pelagica

Date of Sighting _____

Location of Sighting _____

_____

Notes _____

_____

_____

_____

_____

_____

_____

_____

_____

_____

_____

Common Swift
Apus apus

Date of Sighting _____

Location of Sighting _____

_____

Notes _____

_____

_____

_____

_____

_____

_____

_____

White-collared Swift
Streptoprocne zonaris

Date of Sighting

Location of Sighting

Notes

White-throated Swift
Aeronautes saxatalis

Date of Sighting

Location of Sighting

Notes

White-throated Needletail
Hirundapus caudacutus

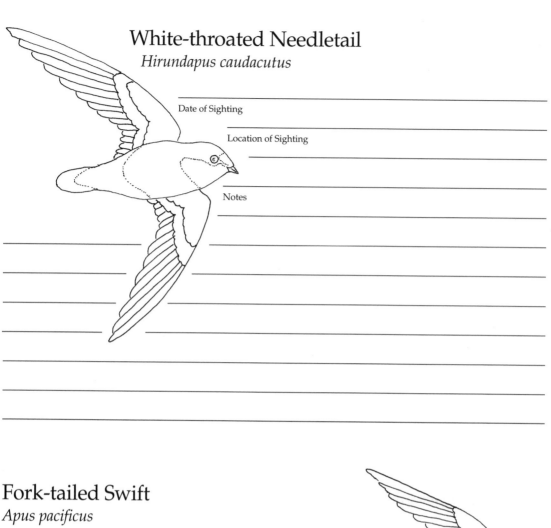

Date of Sighting

Location of Sighting

Notes

Fork-tailed Swift
Apus pacificus

Date of Sighting

Location of Sighting

Notes

Hummingbirds

(family Trochilidae)

When describing hummingbirds one is compelled to list a string of amazing facts. Their wings beat about eighty times each second. They consume about half their body weight in nectar each day, plus a few bugs. (That means at eight pounds per gallon, you and I would have to slurp down about nine to ten gallons of sugar water each day, plus a few bugs.) My favorite hummingbird fact: A hummingbird can be mailed anywhere in the United States for the price of a first-class stamp; most hummingbirds weigh less than one ounce.

Green Violet-ear
Colibri thalassinus

Date of Sighting

Location of Sighting

Notes

Green-breasted Mango
Anthracothorax prevostii

Date of Sighting

Location of Sighting

Notes

Buff-bellied Hummingbird
Amazilia yucatanensis

Date of Sighting

Location of Sighting

Notes

Berylline Hummingbird
Amazilia beryllina

Date of Sighting

Location of Sighting

Notes

Bahama Woodstar

Calliphlox evelynae

Date of Sighting

Location of Sighting

Notes

Violet-crowned
Hummingbird

Amazilia violiceps

Date of Sighting

Location of Sighting

Notes

Lucifer Hummingbird
Calothorax lucifer

Date of Sighting

Location of Sighting

Notes

Broad-billed Hummingbird
Cynanthus latirostris

Date of Sighting

Location of Sighting

Notes

White-eared Hummingbird
Hylocharis leucotis

Date of Sighting

Location of Sighting

Notes

Blue-throated Hummingbird
Lampornis clemenciae

Date of Sighting

Location of Sighting

Notes

Xantus's Hummingbird
Hylocharis xantusii

Date of Sighting

Location of Sighting

Notes

_____

_____

_____

_____

_____

_____

_____

_____

Magnificent Hummingbird
Eugenes fulgens

Date of Sighting

Location of Sighting

Notes

_____

_____

_____

_____

_____

_____

_____

Plain-capped Starthroat
Heliomaster constantii

Date of Sighting

Location of Sighting

Notes

Ruby-throated Hummingbird
Archilochus colubris

Date of Sighting

Location of Sighting

Notes

Black-chinned Hummingbird
Archilochus alexandri

Date of Sighting

Location of Sighting

Notes

Costa's Hummingbird
Calypte costae

Date of Sighting

Location of Sighting

Notes

Anna's Hummingbird
Calypte anna

Date of Sighting

Location of Sighting

Notes

Broad-tailed Hummingbird
Selasphorus platycercus

Date of Sighting

Location of Sighting

Notes

Calliope Hummingbird
Stellula calliope

Date of Sighting

Location of Sighting

Notes

Rufous Hummingbird
Selasphorus rufus

Date of Sighting

Location of Sighting

Notes

Allen's Hummingbird
Selasphorus sasin

Date of Sighting

Location of Sighting

Notes

Trogons
(family Trogonidae)

Probably the most recognized trogon is the Resplendent Quetzel, the emerald green and ruby red messenger of the Aztec gods of Mexico and Central America. Resplendent is descriptive, but it understates the magical beauty of these forest birds. In North America, we can see two exquisite members of this family, both in Arizona.

Elegant Trogon
Trogon elegans

Date of Sighting

Location of Sighting

Notes

Eared Trogon
Euptilotis neoxenus

Date of Sighting

Location of Sighting

Notes

Kingfishers
(family Alcedinidae)

Kingfishers seem to be spirited, energetic, and cranky by nature. I once had to punch my kayak through skim-ice frosting the shore of the Potomac River to get to the open water. When I returned a couple hours later, a Belted Kingfisher had staked out the open water I had created. It became incensed when I approached and harshly scolded me, doing its best to drive me away from its fishing spot. This is the closest look I have ever had of this feisty bird. We can see the plucky bird throughout the United States.

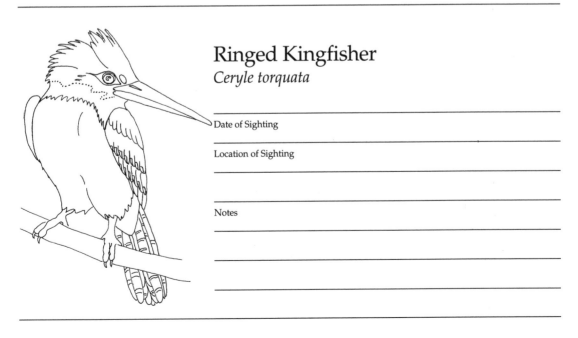

Belted Kingfisher
Ceryle alcyon

Date of Sighting

Location of Sighting

Notes

Ringed Kingfisher
Ceryle torquata

Date of Sighting

Location of Sighting

Notes

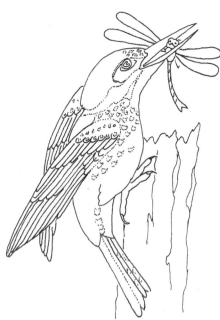

Green Kingfisher
Chloroceryle americana

Date of Sighting

Location of Sighting

Notes

Woodpeckers

(family Picidae)

Most woodpeckers are very natty, formal dressers, sporting basic black with at least some red on the head. Only a few of our woodpeckers are brown, including the Arizona Woodpecker, formerly the Strickland's Woodpecker. Most woodpeckers are found on trees, usually feeding on insects found in the bark or excavating nesting holes in the softer dead wood. The Northern Flicker, a golden-brown woodpecker, is a ground feeder, eating mainly ants. We can hear woodpecker churls and haunting calls in practically every woodland habitat in North America.

Red-headed Woodpecker
Melanerpes erythrocephalus

Date of Sighting

Location of Sighting

Notes

Acorn Woodpecker
Melanerpes formicivorus

Date of Sighting

Location of Sighting

Notes

White-headed Woodpecker
Picoides albolarvatus

Date of Sighting

Location of Sighting

Notes

Lewis's Woodpecker
Melanerpes lewis

Date of Sighting

Location of Sighting

Notes

Golden-fronted Woodpecker
Melanerpes aurifrons

Date of Sighting

Location of Sighting

Notes

Red-bellied Woodpecker
Melanerpes carolinus

Date of Sighting

Location of Sighting

Notes

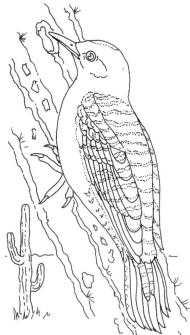

Gila Woodpecker
Melanerpes uropygialis

Date of Sighting

Location of Sighting

Notes

Northern Flicker
Colaptes auratus

Date of Sighting

Location of Sighting

Notes

Gilded Flicker
Colaptes chrysoides

Date of Sighting

Location of Sighting

Notes

Williamson's Sapsucker
Sphyrapicus thyroideus

Date of Sighting

Location of Sighting

Notes

Red-breasted Sapsucker
Sphyrapicus ruber

Date of Sighting

Location of Sighting

Notes

Yellow-bellied Sapsucker
Sphyrapicus varius

Date of Sighting

Location of Sighting

Notes

Red-naped Sapsucker

Sphyrapicus nuchalis

Date of Sighting

Location of Sighting

Notes

Ladder-backed Woodpecker

Picoides scalaris

Date of Sighting

Location of Sighting

Notes

Red-cockaded Woodpecker
Picoides borealis

Date of Sighting

Location of Sighting

Notes

Nuttall's Woodpecker
Picoides nuttallii

Date of Sighting

Location of Sighting

Notes

Arizona Woodpecker
Picoides arizonae

Date of Sighting

Location of Sighting

Notes

Downy Woodpecker
Picoides pubescens

Date of Sighting

Location of Sighting

Notes

Hairy Woodpecker
Picoides villosus

Date of Sighting

Location of Sighting

Notes

Three-toed Woodpecker
Picoides tridactylus

Date of Sighting

Location of Sighting

Notes

Black-backed Woodpecker
Picoides arcticus

Date of Sighting

Location of Sighting

Notes

Ivory-billed Woodpecker
Campephilus principalis

Date of Sighting

Location of Sighting

Notes

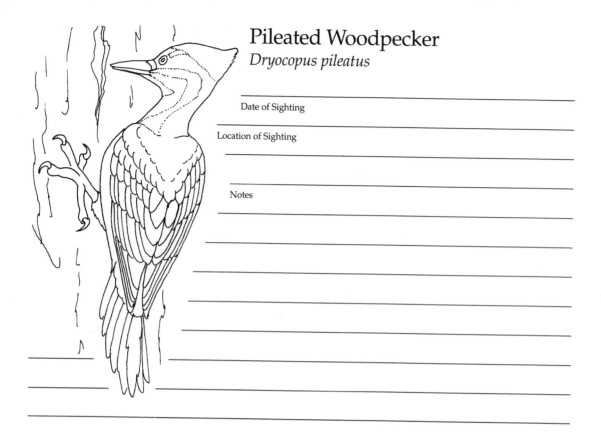

Pileated Woodpecker
Dryocopus pileatus

Date of Sighting

Location of Sighting

Notes

Tyrant Flycatchers
(family Tyrannidae)

Know the voice, know the bird. Sometimes, it's the only way. My favorite Tyrannidae moment occurred in Dyke Marsh along the western shore of the Potomac River just south of Washington, D.C. I met an excited birder coming off the trail just as I was entering; he told me a Willow Flycatcher was perched on the left side of the trail singing its heart out. I rushed ahead and the bird was still there, singing its *fitz-bew*, *fitz-bew* song right out of the field guide. Hearing that characteristic sound is the only surefire way to tell the Willow Flycatcher from the Alder. Another lifer. I just love birdwatching.

Greater Pewee
Contopus pertinax

Date of Sighting

Location of Sighting

Notes

Olive-sided Flycatcher
Contopus cooperi

Date of Sighting

Location of Sighting

Notes

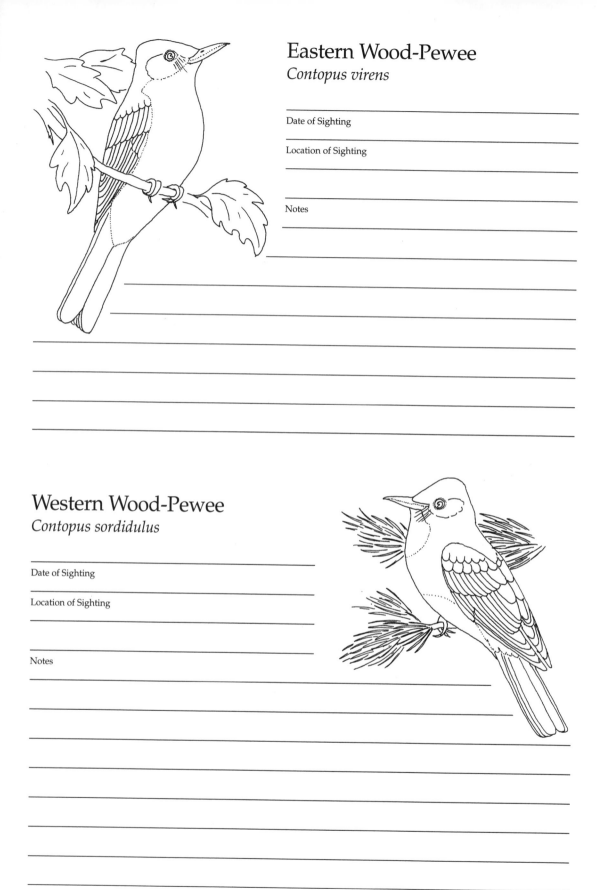

Eastern Wood-Pewee
Contopus virens

Date of Sighting

Location of Sighting

Notes

Western Wood-Pewee
Contopus sordidulus

Date of Sighting

Location of Sighting

Notes

Cuban Pewee
Contopus caribaeus

Date of Sighting
_____

Location of Sighting
_____

Notes
_____
_____
_____
_____
_____

_____
_____
_____
_____

Acadian Flycatcher
Empidonax virescens

Date of Sighting
_____

Location of Sighting
_____

Notes
_____
_____
_____
_____
_____

_____
_____
_____
_____

Yellow-bellied Flycatcher
Empidonax flaviventris

Date of Sighting

Location of Sighting

Notes

Alder Flycatcher
Empidonax alnorum

Date of Sighting

Location of Sighting

Notes

Willow Flycatcher
Empidonax traillii

Date of Sighting

Location of Sighting

Notes

Least Flycatcher
Empidonax minimus

Date of Sighting

Location of Sighting

Notes

Hammond's Flycatcher
Empidonax hammondii

Date of Sighting

Location of Sighting

Notes

Gray Flycatcher
Empidonax wrightii

Date of Sighting

Location of Sighting

Notes

Dusky Flycatcher
Empidonax oberholseri

Date of Sighting

Location of Sighting

Notes

Pacific-slope Flycatcher
Empidonax difficilis

Date of Sighting

Location of Sighting

Notes

Cordilleran Flycatcher
Empidonax occidentalis

Date of Sighting

Location of Sighting

Notes

Buff-breasted Flycatcher
Empidonax fulvifrons

Date of Sighting

Location of Sighting

Notes

Northern Beardless-Tyrannulet
Camptostoma imberbe

Date of Sighting

Location of Sighting

Notes

Eastern Phoebe
Sayornis phoebe

Date of Sighting

Location of Sighting

Notes

Black Phoebe
Sayornis nigricans

Date of Sighting _____

Location of Sighting _____

Notes _____

_____

_____

_____

_____

_____

_____

_____

_____

Say's Phoebe
Sayornis saya

Date of Sighting _____

Location of Sighting _____

Notes _____

_____

_____

_____

_____

_____

_____

_____

Vermillion Flycatcher
Pyrocephalus rubinus

Date of Sighting

Location of Sighting

Notes

Brown-crested Flycatcher
Myiarchus tyrannulus

Date of Sighting

Location of Sighting

Notes

Great Crested Flycatcher
Myiarchus crinitus

Date of Sighting

Location of Sighting

Notes

Nutting's Flycatcher
Myiarchus nuttingi

Date of Sighting

Location of Sighting

Notes

Ash-throated Flycatcher
Myiarchus cinerascens

Date of Sighting

Location of Sighting

Notes

La Sagra's Flycatcher
Myiarchus sagrae

Date of Sighting

Location of Sighting

Notes

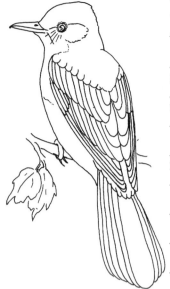

Dusky-capped Flycatcher
Myiarchus tuberculifer

Date of Sighting

Location of Sighting

Notes

Western Kingbird
Tyrannus verticalis

Date of Sighting

Location of Sighting

Notes

Cassin's Kingbird
Tyrannus vociferans

Date of Sighting

Location of Sighting

Notes

Tropical Kingbird
Tyrannus melancholicus

Date of Sighting

Location of Sighting

Notes

Couch's Kingbird
Tyrannus couchii

Date of Sighting

Location of Sighting

Notes

Fork-tailed Flycatcher
Tyrannus savana

Date of Sighting

Location of Sighting

Notes

Eastern Kingbird
Tyrannus tyrannus

Date of Sighting

Location of Sighting

Notes

Loggerhead Kingbird
Tyrannus caudifasciatus

Date of Sighting

Location of Sighting

Notes

Gray Kingbird
Tyrannus dominicensis

Date of Sighting

Location of Sighting

Notes

Thick-billed Kingbird
Tyrannus crassirostris

Date of Sighting

Location of Sighting

Notes

Scissor-tailed Flycatcher
Tyrannus forficatus

Date of Sighting

Location of Sighting

Notes

Piratic Flycatcher
Legatus leucophaius

Date of Sighting

Location of Sighting

Notes

Variegated Flycatcher
Empidonomus varius

Date of Sighting

Location of Sighting

Notes

Great Kiskadee
Pitangus sulphuratus

Date of Sighting

Location of Sighting

Notes

Sulphur-bellied Flycatcher
Myiodynastes luteiventris

Date of Sighting

Location of Sighting

Notes

Rose-throated Becard
Pachyramphus aglaiae

Date of Sighting

Location of Sighting

Notes

Shrikes
(family Laniidae)

Shrikes are songbirds with the attitude of falcons. They hunt by swooping down on their prey, usually large insects, but quite often small birds and mice. They kill by snapping the necks of their victims with a hard crunch of their hooked and notched beaks. Shrikes are also called "larder birds" for their habit of storing prey on thorns or barbed wire to eat later. The Northern Shrike and Loggerhead Shrike look like the Northern Mockingbird but have a well-defined black mask and tell-tale hooked beak.

Brown Shrike
Lanius cristatus

Date of Sighting

Location of Sighting

Notes

Loggerhead Shrike
Lanius ludovicianus

Date of Sighting

Location of Sighting

Notes

Northern Shrike
Lanius excubitor

Date of Sighting

Location of Sighting

Notes

Vireos
(family Vireonidae)

Vireos tend to stay deep in the foliage and out of sight, making them a difficult family of birds to see. They love to sing, however, so it is often possible to locate them by sound, and then coax them into view by pishing. Vireos sing throughout the day, even after other birds have fallen silent, and their songs are endlessly repetitive. I once spotted a White-eyed Vireo in the eastern Texas scrubland that jumped to the front of its thicket just to scold me for getting too close.

Black-capped Vireo
Vireo atricapillus

Date of Sighting

Location of Sighting

Notes

White-eyed Vireo
Vireo griseus

Date of Sighting

Location of Sighting

Notes

Thick-billed Vireo
Vireo crassirostris

Date of Sighting

Location of Sighting

Notes

Yellow-throated Vireo
Vireo flavifrons

Date of Sighting

Location of Sighting

Notes

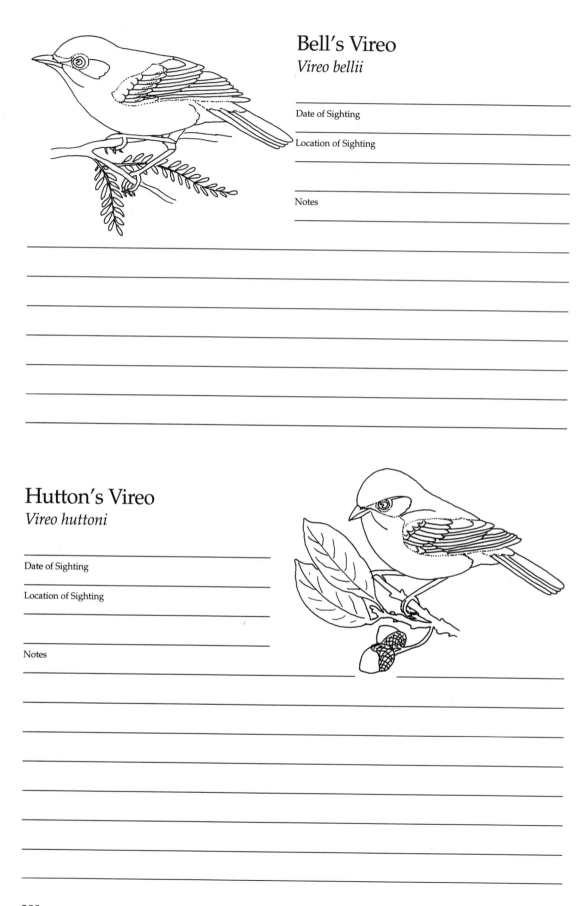

Bell's Vireo
Vireo bellii

Date of Sighting

Location of Sighting

Notes

Hutton's Vireo
Vireo huttoni

Date of Sighting

Location of Sighting

Notes

Gray Vireo
Vireo vicinior

Date of Sighting

Location of Sighting

Notes

Blue-headed Vireo
Vireo solitarius

Date of Sighting

Location of Sighting

Notes

Plumbeous Vireo
Vireo plumbeus

Date of Sighting

Location of Sighting

Notes

Cassin's Vireo
Vireo cassinii

Date of Sighting

Location of Sighting

Notes

Yellow-green Vireo
Vireo flavoviridis

Date of Sighting

Location of Sighting

Notes

Red-eyed Vireo
Vireo olivaceus

Date of Sighting

Location of Sighting

Notes

Black-whiskered Vireo
Vireo altiloquus

Date of Sighting

Location of Sighting

Notes

Philadelphia Vireo
Vireo philadelphicus

Date of Sighting

Location of Sighting

Notes

Warbling Vireo
Vireo gilvus

Date of Sighting

Location of Sighting

Notes

Jays and Crows
(family Corvidae)

Despite the wise old owl's reputation, corvids may be the smartest of all the families of birds. A corvid's brain, the size of a walnut, is larger for its body size than is ours. Crows have been observed placing nuts in the street for passing cars to crack open. We know crows can count, possibly up to five, and love to play games, such as dropping a stick, then diving to catch it before it hits the ground. Crows and jays are a boisterous and bold family with strong, large beaks; they eat almost everything, from berries and nuts to eggs and baby birds, even to carrion. They may be hard to love, but you have to appreciate their strong survival instincts and industrious nature.

Blue Jay
Cyanocitta cristata

Date of Sighting

Location of Sighting

Notes

Steller's Jay
Cyanocitta stelleri

Date of Sighting

Location of Sighting

Notes

Gray Jay
Perisoreus canadensis

Date of Sighting

Location of Sighting

Notes

Clark's Nutcracker
Nucifraga columbiana

Date of Sighting

Location of Sighting

Notes

Western Scrub Jay
Aphelocoma californica

Date of Sighting

Location of Sighting

Notes

Island Scrub Jay
Aphelocoma insularis

Date of Sighting

Location of Sighting

Notes

296

Florida Scrub Jay
Aphelocoma coerulescens

Date of Sighting
_____

Location of Sighting
_____

_____

Notes
_____

_____

_____

_____

_____

_____

Mexican Jay
Aphelocoma ultramarina

Date of Sighting
_____

Location of Sighting
_____

_____

Notes
_____

Pinyon Jay
Gymnorhinus cyanocephalus

Date of Sighting

Location of Sighting

Notes

Brown Jay
Cyanocorax morio

Date of Sighting

Location of Sighting

Notes

Green Jay
Cyanocorax yncas

_____

Date of Sighting

_____

Location of Sighting

_____

_____

Notes

_____

_____

_____

_____

_____

_____

_____

_____

Black-billed Magpie
Pica hudsonia

_____

Date of Sighting

_____

Location of Sighting

_____

_____

Notes

_____

_____

_____

_____

_____

Yellow-billed Magpie
Pica nuttalli

Date of Sighting

Location of Sighting

Notes

Eurasian Jackdaw
Corvus monedula

Date of Sighting

Location of Sighting

Notes

Tamaulipas Crow
Corvus imparatus

Date of Sighting

Location of Sighting

Notes

American Crow
Corvus brachyrhynchos

Date of Sighting

Location of Sighting

Notes

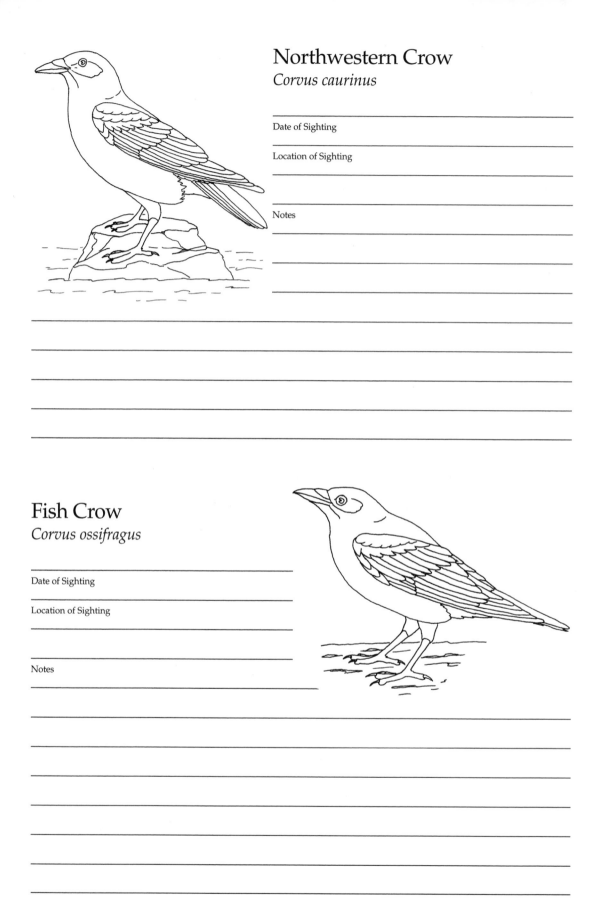

Northwestern Crow
Corvus caurinus

Date of Sighting

Location of Sighting

Notes

Fish Crow
Corvus ossifragus

Date of Sighting

Location of Sighting

Notes

Chihuahuan Raven
Corvus cryptoleucus

Date of Sighting

Location of Sighting

Notes

Common Raven
Corvus corax

Date of Sighting

Location of Sighting

Notes

Larks

(family Alaudidae)

Wе have two larks in North America: the small introduced population of Sky Larks near Vancouver and the ubiquitous Horned Lark. Both are ground nesters and feeders. The Horned Lark is often visible near open farm fields. From a distance, it is just another dun-colored sparrowlike bird, but once you see one through your binoculars, you will never forget the formal elegance of this lovely creature.

Sky Lark
Alauda arvensis

Date of Sighting

Location of Sighting

Notes

Horned Lark
Eremophila alpestris

Date of Sighting

Location of Sighting

Notes

Swallows
(family Hirundinidae)

Swallows are almost exclusively aerial feeders and among the most graceful fliers of all the songbirds. At a small lake near my neighborhood, Barn Swallows gather to feed every summer evening. I regularly watch them buzz the lake, skimming bugs off the surface, then pull almost straight up and engage in a series of climbs, hairpin turns, stalls, and loops. It looks like they are just having fun. The largest swallow in North America, and perhaps our most popular one, is the Purple Martin. This social bird has accommodated itself to human populations so completely that it is almost totally dependent upon man-made housing for its nesting requirements.

Tree Swallow
Tachycineta bicolor

Date of Sighting

Location of Sighting

Notes

Bahama Swallow
Tachycineta cyaneoviridis

Date of Sighting

Location of Sighting

Notes

Violet-green Swallow
Tachycineta thalassina

Date of Sighting

Location of Sighting

Notes

Purple Martin
Progne subis

Date of Sighting

Location of Sighting

Notes

Common House-Martin
Delichon urbica

Date of Sighting

Location of Sighting

Notes

Bank Swallow
Riparia riparia

Date of Sighting

Location of Sighting

Notes

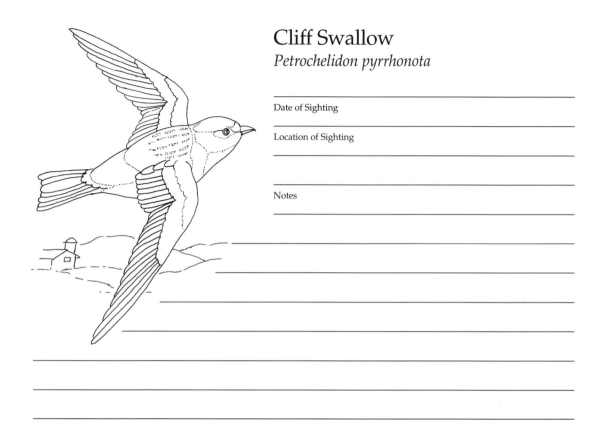

Cliff Swallow
Petrochelidon pyrrhonota

Date of Sighting

Location of Sighting

Notes

Northern Rough-winged Swallow
Stelgidopteryx serripennis

Date of Sighting

Location of Sighting

Notes

Barn Swallow
Hirundo rustica

Date of Sighting

Location of Sighting

Notes

Cave Swallow
Petrochelidon fulva

Date of Sighting

Location of Sighting

Notes

Babblers

(family Timaliidae)

We have only one babbler in North America, the Wrentit, and a curious bird it is. Not only does this songbird not migrate; it may spend its entire life within a tiny two-acre area. You can see the Wrentit only on the west coast.

Wrentit

Chamaea fasciata

Date of Sighting

Location of Sighting

Notes

Titmice and Chickadees
(family Paridae)

Most members of this family of social, spirited birds do not migrate, readily visiting backyard feeders all year, even during the toughest winters.

Bridled Titmouse
Baeolophus wollweberi

Date of Sighting

Location of Sighting

Notes

Oak Titmouse
Baeolophus inortatus

Date of Sighting

Location of Sighting

Notes

Juniper Titmouse
Baeolophus griseus

Date of Sighting

Location of Sighting

Notes

Tufted Titmouse
Baeolophus bicolor

Date of Sighting

Location of Sighting

Notes

Black-capped Chickadee
Poecile atricapillus

Date of Sighting

Location of Sighting

Notes

Carolina Chickadee
Poecile carolinensis

Date of Sighting

Location of Sighting

Notes

Mexican Chickadee
Poecile sclateri

Date of Sighting

Location of Sighting

Notes

Mountain Chickadee
Poecile gambeli

Date of Sighting

Location of Sighting

Notes

314

Chestnut-backed Chickadee
Poecile rufescens

Date of Sighting

Location of Sighting

Notes

Gray-headed Chickadee
Poecile cinctus

Date of Sighting

Location of Sighting

Notes

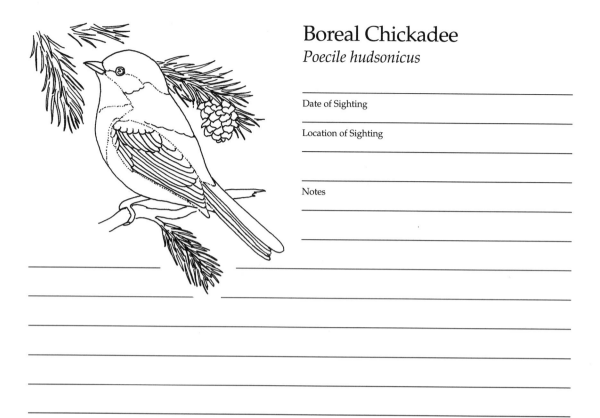

Boreal Chickadee
Poecile hudsonicus

Date of Sighting

Location of Sighting

Notes

Verdins
(family Remizidae)

Previously thought to be related to chickadees, this tiny desert dweller is now assigned to its own family. The Verdin has the curious habit of building several nests each year, some constructed solely to provide protection from cold desert nights. A constantly active little bird, the Verdin feeds mainly on insects in desert scrub and small bushes. It has also been known to visit hummingbird feeders to feast on the sugar water.

Verdin
Auriparus flaviceps

Date of Sighting

Location of Sighting

Notes

Bushtits
(family Aegithalidae)

This tiny, active gray bird seems to be always described as "inconspicuous." It feeds in large flocks, which often move around so quietly that the entire flock may go unnoticed until it leaves to move to another feeding site. The Bushtit looks like a chickadee but has a noticeably longer tail. It is found in the Southwest and along the Pacific coast.

Bushtit
Psaltriparus minimus

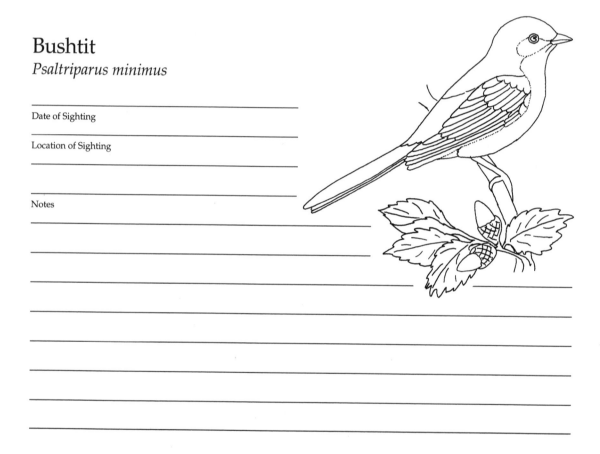

Date of Sighting

Location of Sighting

Notes

Creepers
(family Certhiidae)

The Brown Creeper, our only creeper, spends most of its time climbing from the base of a tree to the top, searching for small insects. Because it blends in so well with tree bark and because it spends so little time in flight, the Brown Creeper is very difficult to spot. In fact, most of the flying it does is from the top of one tree to the base of another. Throughout North America, creepers can be found in open, mature woods, creeping up trees like stiff-tailed miniature woodpeckers or tree-climbing mice with wings.

Brown Creeper
Certhia americana

Date of Sighting

Location of Sighting

Notes

Nuthatches

(family Sittidae)

Our four nuthatches have sharp toenails and strong feet that they use to walk straight up, straight down, and all around tree trunks and branches, like fearless little circus stars. Unlike woodpeckers and the Brown Creeper, nuthatches do not use their tails as braces as they maneuver over the bark in search of insects. They are common backyard feeders that willingly nest in any convenient birdhouse.

White-breasted Nuthatch
Sitta carolinensis

Date of Sighting

Location of Sighting

Notes

Red-breasted Nuthatch
Sitta canadensis

Date of Sighting

Location of Sighting

Notes

Pygmy Nuthatch
Sitta pygmaea

Date of Sighting

Location of Sighting

Notes

Brown-headed Nuthatch
Sitta pusilla

Date of Sighting

Location of Sighting

Notes

Wrens

(family Troglodytidae)

Wrens are an energetic family of small brown birds, typically found skittering through low bush and leaf litter with their tails lifted high above their backs, frantically searching for insects. The exception is the big Cactus Wren, usually found perching on and nesting in cactus plants in the desert Southwest. Wrens are easily enticed to backyard feeders and readily nest in an appropriate birdhouse.

House Wren
Troglodytes aedon

Date of Sighting

Location of Sighting

Notes

Winter Wren
Troglodytes troglodytes

Date of Sighting

Location of Sighting

Notes

Carolina Wren
Thryothorus ludovicianus

Date of Sighting

Location of Sighting

Notes

Bewick's Wren
Thryomanes bewickii

Date of Sighting

Location of Sighting

Notes

Cactus Wren
Campylorhynchus brunneicapillus

Date of Sighting

Location of Sighting

Notes

Rock Wren
Salpinctes obsoletus

Date of Sighting

Location of Sighting

Notes

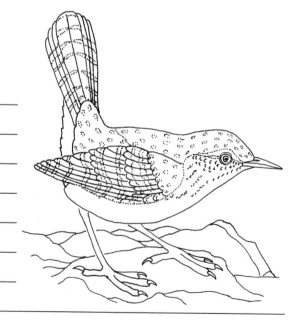

Canyon Wren
Catherpes mexicanus

Date of Sighting

Location of Sighting

Notes

Marsh Wren
Cistothorus palustris

Date of Sighting

Location of Sighting

Notes

Sedge Wren
Cistothorus platensis

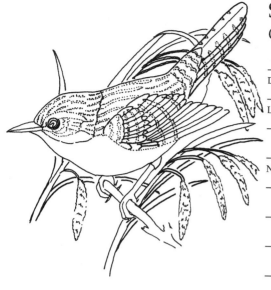

Date of Sighting

Location of Sighting

Notes

Dippers
(family Cinclidae)

These amazing little gray songbirds feed by propelling themselves with their wings through fast-moving mountain streams, swimming to the bottom, and probing under rocks for aquatic insects.

American Dipper
Cinclus mexicanus

Date of Sighting

Location of Sighting

Notes

Kinglets
(family Regulidae)

Kinglets are among the smallest birds in North America, usually seen during spring migration as they clamber around small tree branches looking for food. The yellow head-stripe of the Golden-crowned Kinglet is usually quite noticeable, but the red head-stripe of the Ruby-crowned Kinglet is visible only when the bird is agitated.

Golden-crowned Kinglet
Regulus satrapa

Date of Sighting
_____

Location of Sighting
_____
_____

Notes
_____
_____
_____

Ruby-crowned Kinglet
Regulus calendula

Date of Sighting
_____

Location of Sighting
_____
_____

Notes
_____
_____
_____

Gnatcatchers and Old World Warblers

(family Sylviidae)

The feisty Blue-gray Gnatcatcher is the most common and widespread member of this family. You will most likely hear its grinding buzz from high in the canopy, as the bird busily searches for insects. The gnatcatcher is an ordinary-looking bird until you get it in your binoculars; then you can see the lovely subtleties of its muted colors.

Blue-gray Gnatcatcher
Polioptila caerulea

Date of Sighting

Location of Sighting

Notes

Black-capped Gnatcatcher
Polioptila nigriceps

Date of Sighting

Location of Sighting

Notes

Black-tailed Gnatcatcher
Polioptila melanura

Date of Sighting

Location of Sighting

Notes

California Gnatcatcher
Polioptila californica

Date of Sighting

Location of Sighting

Notes

Lanceolated Warbler
Locustella lanceolata

Date of Sighting

Location of Sighting

Notes

Middendorff's Grasshopper-Warbler
Locustella ochotensis

Date of Sighting

Location of Sighting

Notes

Dusky Warbler
Phylloscopus fuscatus

Date of Sighting

Location of Sighting

Notes

Arctic Warbler
Phylloscopus borealis

Date of Sighting

Location of Sighting

Notes

Old World Flycatchers

(family Muscicapidae)

The range of this family might be slowly expanding because the members are seen with some regularity in the Aleutians and western Alaska.

Narcissus Flycatcher
Ficedula narcissina

_____

Date of Sighting

_____

Location of Sighting

_____

Notes

_____

_____

_____

_____

Siberian Flycatcher
Muscicapa sibirica

_____

Date of Sighting

_____

Location of Sighting

_____

Notes

_____

_____

_____

333

Red-breasted Flycatcher
Ficedula parva

Date of Sighting

Location of Sighting

Notes

Gray-spotted Flycatcher
Muscicapa griseisticta

Date of Sighting

Location of Sighting

Notes

Asian Brown Flycatcher
Muscicapa dauurica

Date of Sighting

Location of Sighting

Notes

Thrushes

(family Turdidae)

The thrushes are a varied and beautiful family of birds that includes both the blue-birds and the American Robin. Seemingly quite different, these birds reveal their similarities upon close inspection: head shape, beak shape, and a big red breast. Thrushes are generally melodic songsters; go to the southeastern states and spend some time in the woods until you hear the flutelike song of the Wood Thrush. You will be touched.

Siberian Rubythroat
Luscinia calliope

Date of Sighting

Location of Sighting

Notes

Bluethroat
Luscinia svecica

Date of Sighting

Location of Sighting

Notes

Red-flanked Bluetail
Tarsiger cyanurus

Date of Sighting

Location of Sighting

Notes

Northern Wheatear
Oenanthe oenanthe

Date of Sighting

Location of Sighting

Notes

Stonechat
Saxicola torquata

Date of Sighting

Location of Sighting

Notes

Eastern Bluebird
Sialia sialis

Date of Sighting

Location of Sighting

Notes

Western Bluebird
Sialia mexicana

Date of Sighting

Location of Sighting

Notes

Mountain Bluebird
Sialia currucoides

Date of Sighting

Location of Sighting

Notes

Townsend's Solitaire
Myadestes townsendi

Date of Sighting

Location of Sighting

Notes

Wood Thrush
Hylocichla mustelina

Date of Sighting

Location of Sighting

Notes

Veery
Catharus fuscescens

Date of Sighting

Location of Sighting

Notes

Gray-cheeked Thrush
Catharus minimus

Date of Sighting

Location of Sighting

Notes

Bicknell's Thrush
Catharus bicknelli

Date of Sighting

Location of Sighting

Notes

Swainson's Thrush
Catharus ustulatus

Date of Sighting

Location of Sighting

Notes

Hermit Thrush
Catharus guttatus

Date of Sighting

Location of Sighting

Notes

Varied Thrush
Ixoreus naevius

Date of Sighting

Location of Sighting

Notes

343

Eyebrowed Thrush
Turdus obscurus

Date of Sighting _____

Location of Sighting _____

Notes _____

_____

_____

_____

_____

_____

_____

Dusky Thrush
Turdus naumanni

Date of Sighting _____

Location of Sighting _____

Notes

_____

_____

_____

_____

_____

_____

_____

_____

Fieldfare
Turdus pilaris

Date of Sighting

Location of Sighting

Notes

Redwing
Turdus iliacus

Date of Sighting

Location of Sighting

Notes

American Robin
Turdus migratorius

Date of Sighting
_____

Location of Sighting
_____

Notes
_____

_____

_____

_____

_____

White-throated Robin
Turdus assimilis

Date of Sighting
_____

Location of Sighting
_____

Notes
_____

_____

_____

Rufous-backed Robin
Turdus rufopalliatus

Date of Sighting

Location of Sighting

Notes

Clay-colored Robin
Turdus grayi

Date of Sighting

Location of Sighting

Notes

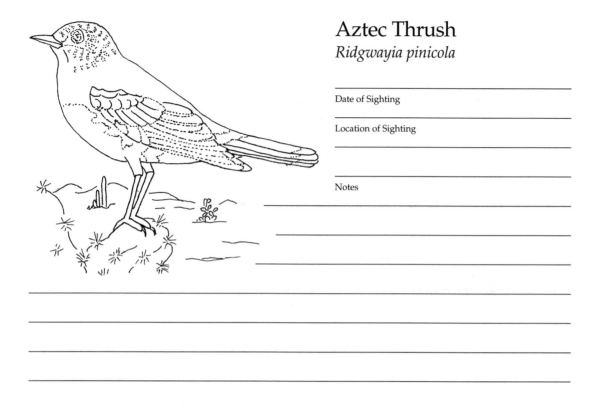

Aztec Thrush
Ridgwayia pinicola

Date of Sighting

Location of Sighting

Notes

Mockingbirds and Thrashers
(family Mimidae)

The mockingbird's song, though incessant, is really quite beautiful. But its behavior isn't so nice. Mockingbirds are very territorial and will attack other birds, cats, dogs, even people who violate the margins of their territory, and only the bird knows exactly where those boundaries are.

Gray Catbird
Dumetella carolinensis

Date of Sighting

Location of Sighting

Notes

Northern Mockingbird
Mimus Polyglottos

Date of Sighting

Location of Sighting

Notes

Bahama Mockingbird
Mimus gundlachii

Date of Sighting

Location of Sighting

Notes

Brown Thrasher
Toxostoma rufum

Date of Sighting

Location of Sighting

Notes

Long-billed Thrasher
Toxostoma longirostre

Date of Sighting

Location of Sighting

Notes

Sage Thrasher
Oreoscoptes montanus

Date of Sighting

Location of Sighting

Notes

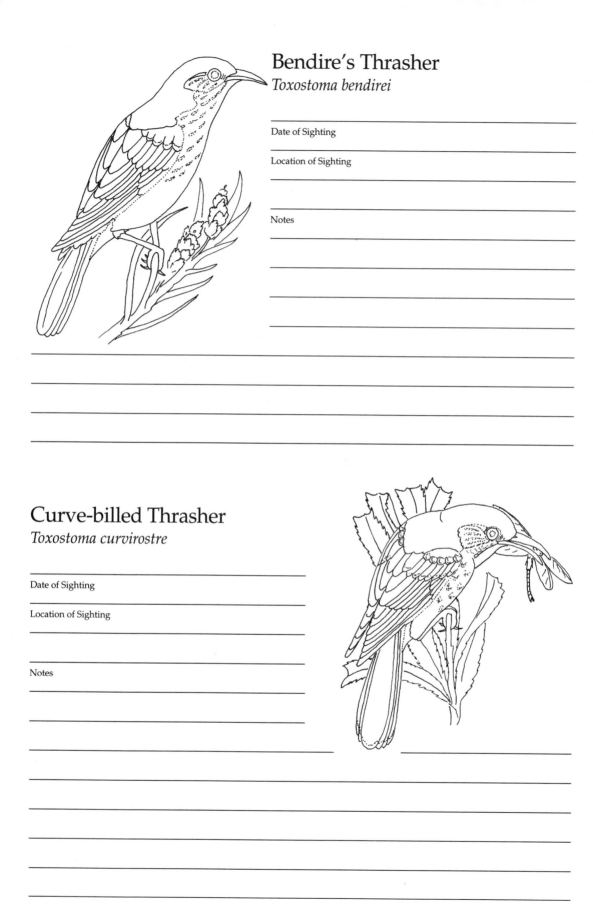

Bendire's Thrasher
Toxostoma bendirei

Date of Sighting

Location of Sighting

Notes

Curve-billed Thrasher
Toxostoma curvirostre

Date of Sighting

Location of Sighting

Notes

California Thrasher
Toxostoma redivivum

Date of Sighting

Location of Sighting

Notes

Crissal Thrasher
Toxostoma crissale

Date of Sighting

Location of Sighting

Notes

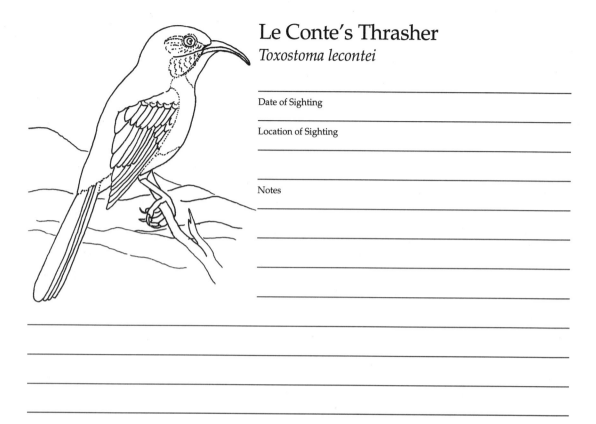

Le Conte's Thrasher
Toxostoma lecontei

Date of Sighting

Location of Sighting

Notes

Starlings

(family Sturnidae)

The European Starling was introduced to North America in the late 1800s and has adapted to its new home so successfully that it is now common throughout the United States, Canada, and northern Mexico. We find the bird somewhat disagreeable because it travels in noisy flocks, is aggressive, and successfully competes for nesting sites with native bluebirds, Red-headed Woodpeckers, and other cavity-nesters. The starling is now being joined with small, established groups of mynas that are close family members.

Crested Myna
Acridotheres cristatellus

Date of Sighting

Location of Sighting

Notes

Common Myna
Acridotheres tristis

Date of Sighting

Location of Sighting

Notes

Hill Myna
Gracula religiosa

Date of Sighting

Location of Sighting

Notes

European Starling
Sturnus vulgaris

Date of Sighting

Location of Sighting

Notes

Accentors
(family Prunellidae)

The Siberian Accentor occurs in North America as a stray from the mountainous regions of Eurasia, appearing not too infrequently in the Aleutians and the interior of Alaska.

Siberian Accentor
Prunella montanella

Date of Sighting

Location of Sighting

Notes

Wagtails and Pipits

(family Motacillidae)

The member of this family most likely to be seen in North America is the American Pipit, a long-legged bird with an erect posture that runs along the ground feeding and bobbing its tail. It sometimes occurs in small flocks.

Yellow Wagtail
Motacilla flava

Date of Sighting

Location of Sighting

Notes

Gray Wagtail
Motacilla cinerea

Date of Sighting

Location of Sighting

Notes

White Wagtail
Motacilla alba

Date of Sighting

Location of Sighting

Notes

Black-backed Wagtail
Motacilla lugens

Date of Sighting

Location of Sighting

Notes

American Pipit
Anthus rubescens

Date of Sighting

Location of Sighting

Notes

Sprague's Pipit
Anthus spragueii

Date of Sighting

Location of Sighting

Notes

Olive-backed Pipit
Anthus hodgsoni

Date of Sighting

Location of Sighting

Notes

Pechora Pipit
Anthus gustavi

Date of Sighting

Location of Sighting

Notes

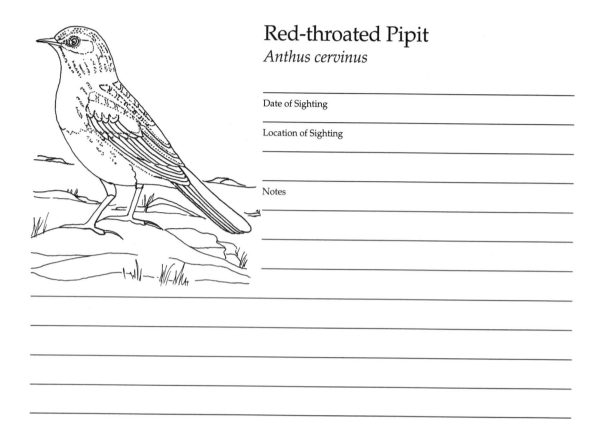

Red-throated Pipit
Anthus cervinus

Date of Sighting

Location of Sighting

Notes

Waxwings
(family Bombycillidae)

Our two waxwings are among the loveliest of North American birds. The Cedar Waxwing, with its sharp crest, black mask, and bright yellow-tipped tail, is more widespread than the Bohemian Waxwing, which is slightly larger and grayer. Waxwings gather in large flocks to feed on berries, often stripping a plant of its fruit before moving on to the next. They are migratory passerines but seem to take slightly different routes each year, so you might not see them in the same area every season.

Bohemian Waxwing
Bombycilla garrulus

Date of Sighting

Location of Sighting

Notes

Cedar Waxwing
Bombycilla cedrorum

Date of Sighting

Location of Sighting

Notes

Silky-Flycatchers
(family Ptilogonatidae)

The Phainopepla looks like a glossy black cardinal but is more closely related to the waxwings. A beautiful desert bird that relishes mistletoe, the Phainopepla also eats other berries and insects. It usually nests in mistletoe too, where its nest is difficult to spot.

Phainopepla
Phainopepla nitens

Date of Sighting

Location of Sighting

Notes

Wood-Warblers
(family Parulidae)

These highly varied and extraordinarily beautiful creatures are truly the ornaments of the bird world. In the spring, when wood-warblers return to North America in their breeding plumage, they are breathtaking gems of color and design. In the autumn, when they return to their wintering grounds, their plumage is monochromatic and dull; they've become what Roger Tory Peterson famously called "confusing fall warblers." The most extraordinary migrant is the Blackpoll Warbler, which every fall flies from the Maine coast nonstop for about seventy-two hours to northern South America.

Prothonotary Warbler
Protonotaria citrea

Date of Sighting

Location of Sighting

Notes

Blue-winged Warbler
Vermivora pinus

Date of Sighting

Location of Sighting

Notes

Golden-winged Warbler
Vermivora chrysoptera

Date of Sighting

Location of Sighting

Notes

Tennessee Warbler
Vermivora peregrina

Date of Sighting

Location of Sighting

Notes

Orange-crowned Warbler
Vermivora celata

Date of Sighting

Location of Sighting

Notes

Bachman's Warbler
Vermivora bachmanii

Date of Sighting

Location of Sighting

Notes

Nashville Warbler
Vermivora ruficapilla

Date of Sighting

Location of Sighting

Notes

Virginia's Warbler
Vermivora virginiae

Date of Sighting

Location of Sighting

Notes

Colima Warbler
Vermivora crissalis

Date of Sighting

Location of Sighting

Notes

Lucy's Warbler
Vermivora luciae

Date of Sighting

Location of Sighting

Notes

Crescent-chested Warbler
Parula superciliosa

Date of Sighting

Location of Sighting

Notes

Northern Parula
Parula americana

Date of Sighting

Location of Sighting

Notes

Tropical Parula
Parula pitiayumi

Date of Sighting

Location of Sighting

Notes

Chestnut-sided Warbler
Dendroica pensylvanica

Date of Sighting

Location of Sighting

Notes

Cape May Warbler
Dendroica tigrina

Date of Sighting

Location of Sighting

Notes

Magnolia Warbler
Dendroica magnolia

Date of Sighting

Location of Sighting

Notes

Yellow-rumped Warbler
Dendroica coronata

Date of Sighting

Location of Sighting

Notes

Black-and-white Warbler
Mniotilta varia

Date of Sighting

Location of Sighting

Notes

Black-throated Blue Warbler
Dendroica caerulescens

Date of Sighting

Location of Sighting

Notes

Cerulean Warbler
Dendroica cerulea

Date of Sighting

Location of Sighting

Notes

Blackburnian Warbler
Dendroica fusca

Date of Sighting

Location of Sighting

Notes

Black-throated Gray Warbler
Dendroica nigrescens

Date of Sighting

Location of Sighting

Notes

Townsend's Warbler
Dendroica townsendi

Date of Sighting

Location of Sighting

Notes

Hermit Warbler
Dendroica occidentalis

Date of Sighting

Location of Sighting

Notes

Black-throated Green Warbler
Dendroica virens

Date of Sighting

Location of Sighting

Notes

Golden-cheeked Warbler
Dendroica chrysoparia

Date of Sighting

Location of Sighting

Notes

Grace's Warbler
Dendroica graciae

Date of Sighting

Location of Sighting

Notes

Yellow-throated Warbler
Dendroica dominica

Date of Sighting

Location of Sighting

Notes

Kirtland's Warbler
Dendroica kirtlandii

Date of Sighting
_____

Location of Sighting
_____

_____

Notes
_____

_____

_____

_____

_____

_____

_____

_____

_____

Prairie Warbler
Dendroica discolor

Date of Sighting
_____

Location of Sighting
_____

_____

Notes
_____

_____

_____

_____

_____

_____

_____

_____

Bay-breasted Warbler
Dendroica castanea

Date of Sighting

Location of Sighting

Notes

Blackpoll Warbler
Dendroica striata

Date of Sighting

Location of Sighting

Notes

Pine Warbler

Dendroica pinus

Date of Sighting

Location of Sighting

Notes

Palm Warbler

Dendroica palmarum

Date of Sighting

Location of Sighting

Notes

Yellow Warbler
Dendroica petechia

Date of Sighting

Location of Sighting

Notes

Mourning Warbler
Oporornis philadelphia

Date of Sighting

Location of Sighting

Notes

MacGillivray's Warbler

Oporornis tolmiei

Date of Sighting

Location of Sighting

Notes

Connecticut Warbler

Oporornis agilis

Date of Sighting

Location of Sighting

Notes

Kentucky Warbler
Oporornis formosus

Date of Sighting

Location of Sighting

Notes

Canada Warbler
Wilsonia canadensis

Date of Sighting

Location of Sighting

Notes

Wilson's Warbler
Wilsonia pusilla

Date of Sighting

Location of Sighting

Notes

Hooded Warbler
Wilsonia citrina

Date of Sighting

Location of Sighting

Notes

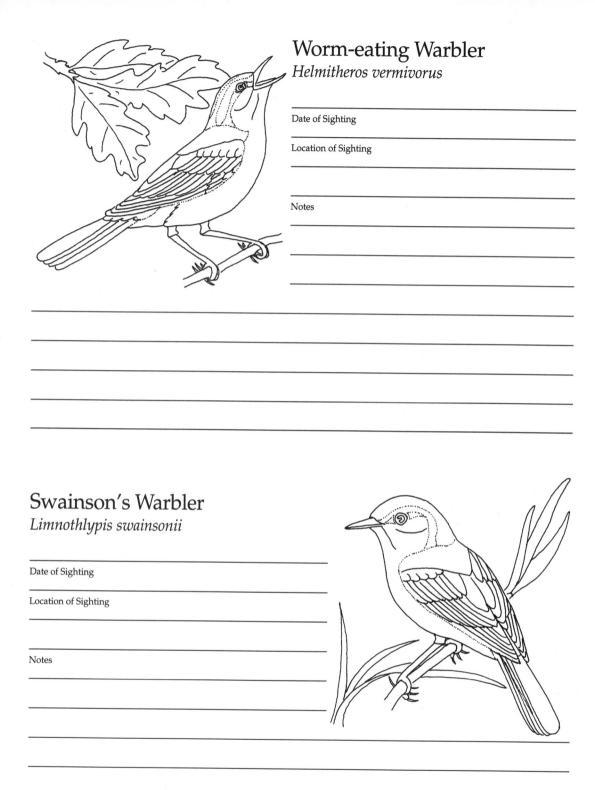

Worm-eating Warbler
Helmitheros vermivorus

Date of Sighting

Location of Sighting

Notes

Swainson's Warbler
Limnothlypis swainsonii

Date of Sighting

Location of Sighting

Notes

Ovenbird
Seiurus aurocapillus

Date of Sighting

Location of Sighting

Notes

Louisiana Waterthrush
Seiurus motacilla

Date of Sighting

Location of Sighting

Notes

Northern Waterthrush
Seiurus noveboracensis

Date of Sighting

Location of Sighting

Notes

Common Yellowthroat
Geothlypis trichas

Date of Sighting

Location of Sighting

Notes

Gray-crowned Yellowthroat
Geothlypis poliocephala

Date of Sighting

Location of Sighting

Notes

Fan-tailed Warbler
Euthlypis lachrymosa

Date of Sighting

Location of Sighting

Notes

Golden-crowned Warbler
Basileuterus culicivorus

Date of Sighting

Location of Sighting

Notes

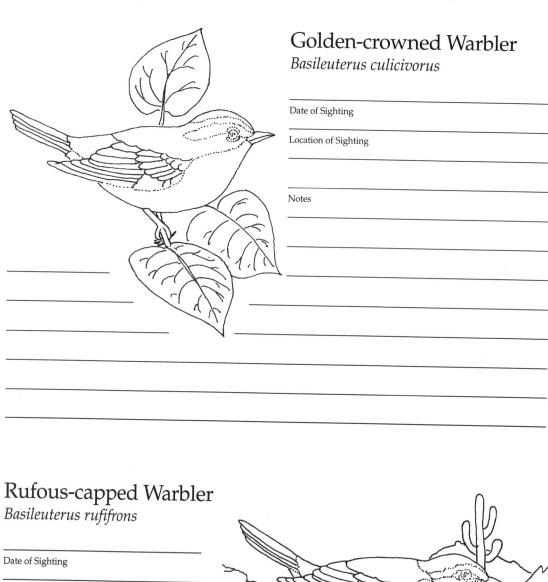

Rufous-capped Warbler
Basileuterus rufifrons

Date of Sighting

Location of Sighting

Notes

Yellow-breasted Chat
Icteria virens

Date of Sighting

Location of Sighting

Notes

American Redstart
Setophaga ruticilla

Date of Sighting

Location of Sighting

Notes

Slate-throated Redstart
Myioborus miniatus

Date of Sighting

Location of Sighting

Notes

Painted Redstart
Myioborus pictus

Date of Sighting

Location of Sighting

Notes

Red-faced Warbler
Cardellina rubrifrons

Date of Sighting

Location of Sighting

Notes

Olive Warblers

(family Peucedramidae)

Recent studies indicate the Olive Warbler may be more closely related to the finches than to the warbler family. Though not uncommon, the Olive Warbler is difficult to spot, as its nests are built thirty to seventy feet high in the trees.

Olive Warbler

Peucedramus taeniatus

Date of Sighting

Location of Sighting

Notes

Tanagers
(family Thraupidae)

The bright, vibrant colors of the tanager family represent the tropics like no other family (except the parrots, of course). Seeing the pure reds and blacks of a Scarlet Tanager for the first time is a startling event. The colors seem too vivid to be real. The best time to spot tanagers is during early spring as they arrive from South America. Once the trees leaf out in late spring and early summer, these brilliantly colored birds are hidden among the canopy leaves.

Summer Tanager
Piranga rubra

Date of Sighting

Location of Sighting

Notes

Hepatic Tanager
Piranga flava

Date of Sighting

Location of Sighting

Notes

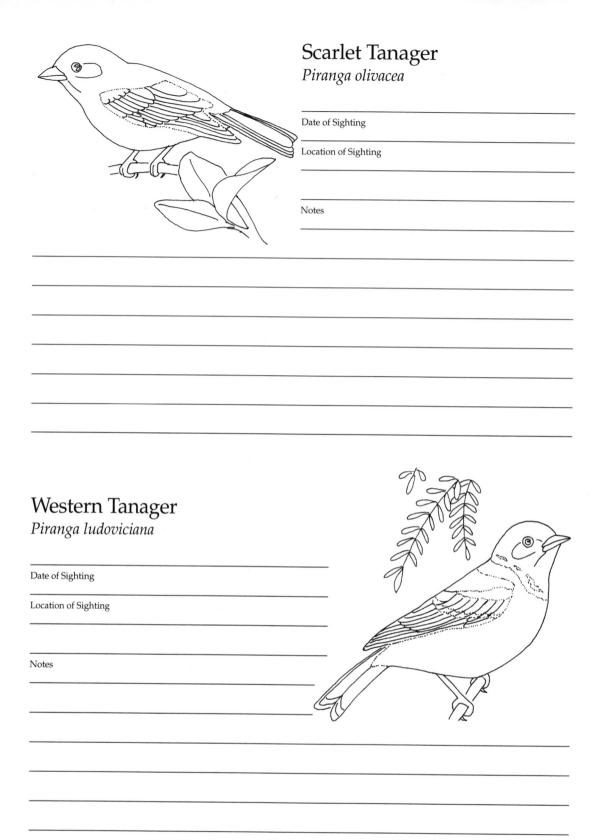

Scarlet Tanager
Piranga olivacea

Date of Sighting

Location of Sighting

Notes

Western Tanager
Piranga ludoviciana

Date of Sighting

Location of Sighting

Notes

Flame-colored Tanager
Piranga bidentata

Date of Sighting

Location of Sighting

Notes

Stripe-headed Tanager
Spindalis zena

Date of Sighting

Location of Sighting

Notes

Bananaquits
(family Coerebidae)

I first saw the Bananaquit on the Yucatan peninsula of Mexico and liked the bird immediately. It is a frenetic little creature, always on the move looking for food. It possesses a slightly decurved beak that it uses to sip nectar from flowers. The Bananaquit is now a regular visitor to southern Florida, where it may soon begin to breed. Scientists think that the Bananaquit is closely related to the tanagers.

Bananaquit
Coereba flaveola

Date of Sighting

Location of Sighting

Notes

Emberizids

(family Emberizidae)

One of my favorite birding experiences was the day I single-handedly positively identified a Field Sparrow. First I heard it sing, then I spotted the little brown bird, which I knew was some kind of sparrow. It was calm and cooperative, and so beautiful through the binoculars. I looked carefully for the field marks; it was the first time I really concentrated on the beauty of sparrows. They have been a favorite of mine ever since.

White-collared Seedeater
Sporophila torqueola

Date of Sighting

Location of Sighting

Notes

Black-faced Grassquit
Tiaris bicolor

Date of Sighting

Location of Sighting

Notes

Yellow-faced Grassquit
Tiaris olivacea

Date of Sighting

Location of Sighting

Notes

Olive Sparrow
Arremonops rufivirgatus

Date of Sighting

Location of Sighting

Notes

Green-tailed Towhee
Pipilo chlorurus

Date of Sighting

Location of Sighting

Notes

California Towhee
Pipilo crissalis

Date of Sighting

Location of Sighting

Notes

Canyon Towhee
Pipilo fuscus

Date of Sighting

Location of Sighting

Notes

Abert's Towhee
Pipilo aberti

Date of Sighting

Location of Sighting

Notes

Eastern Towhee
Pipilo erythrophthalmus

Date of Sighting

Location of Sighting

Notes

Spotted Towhee
Pipilo maculatus

Date of Sighting

Location of Sighting

Notes

Bachman's Sparrow
Aimophila aestivalis

Date of Sighting

Location of Sighting

Notes

Botteri's Sparrow
Aimophila botterii

Date of Sighting

Location of Sighting

Notes

Cassin's Sparrow
Aimophila cassinii

Date of Sighting

Location of Sighting

Notes

Rufous-winged Sparrow
Aimophila carpalis

Date of Sighting

Location of Sighting

Notes

Rufous-crowned Sparrow
Aimophila ruficeps

Date of Sighting

Location of Sighting

Notes

American Tree Sparrow
Spizella arborea

Date of Sighting

Location of Sighting

Notes

Field Sparrow
Spizella pusilla

Date of Sighting

Location of Sighting

Notes

Chipping Sparrow
Spizella passerina

Date of Sighting

Location of Sighting

Notes

Clay-colored Sparrow
Spizella pallida

Date of Sighting

Location of Sighting

Notes

Brewer's Sparrow
Spizella breweri

Date of Sighting

Location of Sighting

Notes

Lark Sparrow
Chondestes grammacus

Date of Sighting

Location of Sighting

Notes

Black-chinned Sparrow
Spizella atrogularis

Date of Sighting

Location of Sighting

Notes

Black-throated Sparrow
Amphispiza bilineata

Date of Sighting

Location of Sighting

Notes

Five-striped Sparrow
Aimophila quinquestriata

Date of Sighting

Location of Sighting

Notes

Sage Sparrow
Amphispiza belli

Date of Sighting

Location of Sighting

Notes

Grasshopper Sparrow
Ammodramus savannarum

Date of Sighting

Location of Sighting

Notes

Baird's Sparrow
Ammodramus bairdii

Date of Sighting

Location of Sighting

Notes

Henslow's Sparrow
Ammodramus henslowii

Date of Sighting

Location of Sighting

Notes

Saltmarsh Sharp-tailed Sparrow
Ammodramus caudacutus

Date of Sighting

Location of Sighting

Notes

Le Conte's Sparrow
Ammodramus leconteii

Date of Sighting

Location of Sighting

Notes

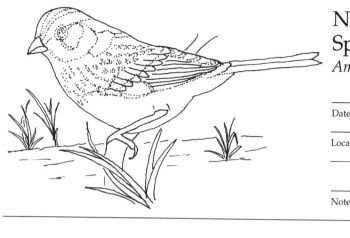

Nelson's Sharp-tailed Sparrow
Ammodramus nelsoni

Date of Sighting

Location of Sighting

Notes

Seaside Sparrow
Ammodramus maritimus

Date of Sighting

Location of Sighting

Notes

Fox Sparrow
Passerella iliaca

Date of Sighting

Location of Sighting

Notes

Lark Bunting
Calamospiza melanocorys

Date of Sighting

Location of Sighting

Notes

Savannah Sparrow
Passerculus sandwichensis

Date of Sighting

Location of Sighting

Notes

Lincoln's Sparrow
Melospiza lincolnii

Date of Sighting

Location of Sighting

Notes

Song Sparrow
Melospiza melodia

Date of Sighting

Location of Sighting

Notes

Vesper Sparrow
Pooecetes gramineus

Date of Sighting

Location of Sighting

Notes

Swamp Sparrow
Melospiza georgiana

Date of Sighting

Location of Sighting

Notes

Harris's Sparrow
Zonotrichia querula

Date of Sighting

Location of Sighting

Notes

White-throated Sparrow
Zonotrichia albicollis

Date of Sighting

Location of Sighting

Notes

White-crowned Sparrow
Zonotrichia leucophrys

Date of Sighting

Location of Sighting

Notes

Golden-crowned Sparrow
Zonotrichia atricapilla

Date of Sighting

Location of Sighting

Notes

Dark-eyed Junco
Junco hyemalis

Date of Sighting

Location of Sighting

Notes

Yellow-eyed Junco
Junco phaeonotus

Date of Sighting

Location of Sighting

Notes

Chestnut-collared Longspur
Calcarius ornatus

Date of Sighting

Location of Sighting

Notes

McCown's Longspur
Calcarius mccownii

Date of Sighting

Location of Sighting

Notes

Smith's Longspur
Calcarius pictus

Date of Sighting

Location of Sighting

Notes

Lapland Longspur
Calcarius lapponicus

Date of Sighting

Location of Sighting

Notes

Snow Bunting
Plectrophenax nivalis

Date of Sighting

Location of Sighting

Notes

McKay's Bunting
Plectrophenax hyperboreus

Date of Sighting

Location of Sighting

Notes

Yellow-breasted Bunting
Emberiza aureola

Date of Sighting

Location of Sighting

Notes

Gray Bunting
Emberiza variabilis

Date of Sighting

Location of Sighting

Notes

Reed Bunting
Emberiza schoeniclus

Date of Sighting

Location of Sighting

Notes

Pallas's Bunting
Emberiza pallasi

Date of Sighting

Location of Sighting

Notes

Little Bunting
Emberiza pusilla

Date of Sighting

Location of Sighting

Notes

Rustic Bunting
Emberiza rustica

Date of Sighting
_____

Location of Sighting
_____

_____

Notes
_____

_____

_____

_____

_____

_____

_____

_____

Cardinals

(family Cardinalidae)

The Northern Cardinal is proof that when we are surrounded by it we can take even extraordinary beauty for granted. I saw a cardinal almost every day near my home in Virginia and, after a time, I came to overlook it. Then I spotted a bright red male perched on a holly branch during a late spring snowstorm and have noticed the bird ever since. The cardinal, along with the other members of the grosbeak family, is a consummate seed-eater, able to crack even the toughest hulls with its big nutcracker-like beak. Cardinals are willing visitors to backyard feeders.

Rose-breasted Grosbeak
Pheucticus ludovicianus

Date of Sighting

Location of Sighting

Notes

Black-headed Grosbeak
Pheucticus melanocephalus

Date of Sighting

Location of Sighting

Notes

Crimson-collared Grosbeak
Rhodothraupis celaeno

Date of Sighting

Location of Sighting

Notes

Yellow Grosbeak
Pheucticus chrysopeplus

Date of Sighting

Location of Sighting

Notes

Northern Cardinal
Cardinalis cardinalis

Date of Sighting

Location of Sighting

Notes

Pyrrhuloxia
Cardinalis sinuatus

Date of Sighting

Location of Sighting

Notes

Dickcissel
Spiza americana

Date of Sighting

_____

Location of Sighting

_____

_____

Notes

_____

_____

_____

_____

_____

_____

_____

_____

Blue Grosbeak
Guiraca caerulea

Date of Sighting

_____

Location of Sighting

_____

_____

Notes

_____

_____

_____

_____

_____

_____

_____

_____

Indigo Bunting
Passerina cyanea

Date of Sighting

Location of Sighting

Notes

Lazuli Bunting
Passerina amoena

Date of Sighting

Location of Sighting

Notes

Painted Bunting
Passerina ciris

Date of Sighting

Location of Sighting

Notes

Varied Bunting
Passerina versicolor

Date of Sighting

Location of Sighting

Notes

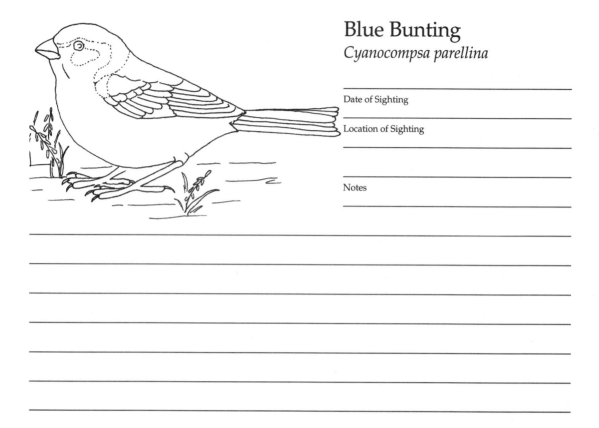

Blue Bunting
Cyanocompsa parellina

Date of Sighting

Location of Sighting

Notes

Blackbirds
(family Icteridae)

My favorite blackbird is the Bobolink, which I first saw during a twenty-four-hour bird-a-thon with my friend Harry Armistead, a black-belt birder who allows me to do secretarial duties for the event. I had told Harry I had never seen a Bobolink, so toward evening he parked beside a sedge field and cut the engine. He was silent. Finally I asked, "What are we doing here?" "Bobolink," Harry replied. About two minutes later Bobolinks in bright breeding plumage began springing from within the sedge like popcorn bouncing from a skillet. They were more beautiful than any photo or illustration I had ever seen. I was mesmerized.

Bobolink
Dolichonyx oryzivorus

Date of Sighting

Location of Sighting

Notes

Eastern Meadowlark
Sturnella magna

Date of Sighting

Location of Sighting

Notes

Western Meadowlark
Sturnella neglecta

Date of Sighting

Location of Sighting

Notes

Yellow-headed Blackbird
Xanthocephalus xanthocephalus

Date of Sighting

Location of Sighting

Notes

Red-winged Blackbird
Agelaius phoeniceus

Date of Sighting

Location of Sighting

Notes

Tricolored Blackbird
Agelaius tricolor

Date of Sighting

Location of Sighting

Notes

Common Grackle
Quiscalus quiscula

Date of Sighting

Location of Sighting

Notes

Boat-tailed Grackle
Quiscalus major

Date of Sighting

Location of Sighting

Notes

Great-tailed Grackle
Quiscalus mexicanus

Date of Sighting

Location of Sighting

Notes

Rusty Blackbird
Euphagus carolinus

Date of Sighting

Location of Sighting

Notes

Brewer's Blackbird
Euphagus cyanocephalus

Date of Sighting

Location of Sighting

Notes

Shiny Cowbird
Molothrus bonariensis

Date of Sighting

Location of Sighting

Notes

Brown-headed Cowbird
Molothrus ater

Date of Sighting

Location of Sighting

Notes

Bronzed Cowbird
Molothrus aeneus

Date of Sighting

Location of Sighting

Notes

Orchard Oriole
Icterus spurius

Date of Sighting

Location of Sighting

Notes

Hooded Oriole
Icterus cucullatus

Date of Sighting

Location of Sighting

Notes

Baltimore Oriole
Icterus galbula

Date of Sighting

Location of Sighting

Notes

Bullock's Oriole
Icterus bullockii

Date of Sighting

Location of Sighting

Notes

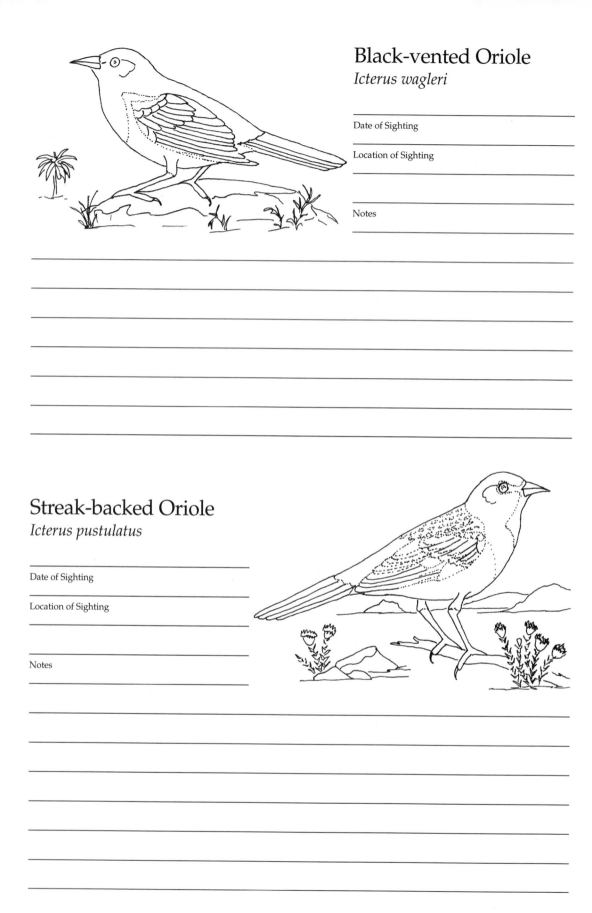

Black-vented Oriole
Icterus wagleri

Date of Sighting

Location of Sighting

Notes

Streak-backed Oriole
Icterus pustulatus

Date of Sighting

Location of Sighting

Notes

Altamira Oriole
Icterus gularis

Date of Sighting

Location of Sighting

Notes

Audubon's Oriole
Icterus graduacauda

Date of Sighting

Location of Sighting

Notes

Spot-breasted Oriole
Icterus pectoralis

Date of Sighting

Location of Sighting

Notes

Scott's Oriole
Icterus parisorum

Date of Sighting

Location of Sighting

Notes

Finches
(family Fringillidae)

Probably the most recognizable member of the finch family is the bright yellow and black American Goldfinch, which many people refer to as a canary. The canary of the cage is in fact related to the finches. Finches are strict vegetarians, preferring seeds and vegetable matter over insects throughout the year. The American Goldfinch prefers black niger thistle seed in a special feeder just for him, and many of us feel his visits are worth the effort.

Oriental Greenfinch
Carduelis sinica

Date of Sighting

Location of Sighting

Notes

Brambling
Fringilla montifringilla

Date of Sighting

Location of Sighting

Notes

Common Chaffinch
Fringilla coelebs

Date of Sighting

Location of Sighting

Notes

Gray-crowned Rosy-Finch
Leucosticte tephrocotis

Date of Sighting

Location of Sighting

Notes

Brown-capped Rosy-Finch
Leucosticte australis

Date of Sighting

Location of Sighting

Notes

Black Rosy-Finch
Leucosticte atrata

Date of Sighting

Location of Sighting

Notes

Purple Finch
Carpodacus purpureus

Date of Sighting

Location of Sighting

Notes

Cassin's Finch
Carpodacus cassinii

Date of Sighting

Location of Sighting

Notes

House Finch
Carpodacus mexicanus

Date of Sighting

Location of Sighting

Notes

Common Rosefinch
Carpodacus erythrinus

Date of Sighting

Location of Sighting

Notes

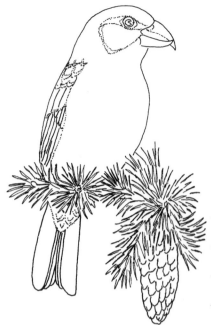

Red Crossbill
Loxia curvirostra

Date of Sighting

Location of Sighting

Notes

White-winged Crossbill
Loxia leucoptera

Date of Sighting

Location of Sighting

Notes

Pine Grosbeak
Pinicola enucleator

Date of Sighting

Location of Sighting

Notes

Pine Siskin
Carduelis pinus

Date of Sighting

Location of Sighting

Notes

American Goldfinch
Carduelis tristis

Date of Sighting

Location of Sighting

Notes

Lesser Goldfinch
Carduelis psaltria

Date of Sighting

Location of Sighting

Notes

Lawrence's Goldfinch
Carduelis lawrencei

Date of Sighting

Location of Sighting

Notes

Common Redpoll
Carduelis flammea

Date of Sighting

Location of Sighting

Notes

Hoary Redpoll
Carduelis hornemanni

Date of Sighting

Location of Sighting

Notes

Evening Grosbeak
Coccothraustes vespertinus

Date of Sighting

Location of Sighting

Notes

Hawfinch
Coccothraustes coccothraustes

Date of Sighting

Location of Sighting

Notes

Eurasian Bullfinch
Pyrrhula pyrrhula

Date of Sighting

Location of Sighting

Notes

Old World Sparrows
(family Passeridae)

The House Sparrow is common throughout the world. Originally from Eurasia and northern Africa, this aggressive, hardy bird is most associated with human activity. You will not find the House Sparrow roughing it in a wilderness environment. Introduced to America in 1851, it now flourishes in all fifty states and throughout subarctic Canada.

House Sparrow
Passer domesticus

Date of Sighting

Location of Sighting

Notes

Eurasian Tree Sparrow
Passer montanus

Date of Sighting

Location of Sighting

Notes

Estrildid Finches

(family Estrildidae)

Small populations of this escaped cage-bird are now firmly established in California and southern Florida. It is too early to tell what impact these pioneer populations will ultimately have on our native species.

Nutmeg Mannikin
Lonchura punctulata

_____
Date of Sighting
_____
Location of Sighting
_____

_____
Notes
_____

_____

_____

_____

_____

_____

_____

_____

Weavers
(family Ploceidae)

The adult male Orange Bishop in breeding plumage is an unmistakable bird. A small population of these escaped cage-birds has been successfully established in southern California; the bird is slowly expanding its range.

Orange Bishop
Euplectes franciscanus

Date of Sighting

Location of Sighting

Notes

INDEX AND CHECKLIST

Alphabetical by Common Name